In a
Different
Voice

In a
Different
Voice

Psychological Theory and Women's Development

Carol Gilligan

Harvard University Press
Cambridge, Massachusetts, and London, England

To my mother and my father

Copyright © 1982 by Carol Gilligan
All rights reserved
Printed in the United States of America

20   19   18   17   16   15

Library of Congress Cataloging in Publication Data

Gilligan, Carol, 1936-
    In a different voice.

    Bibliography: p.
    Includes index.
    1. Women—Psychology—Longitudinal studies.   2. Developmental
psychology—Longitudinal studies.   3. Moral development—Longitudinal
studies.   I. Title.
[DNLM: 1. Women—Psychology.   HQ 1206 G481i]
HQ1206.G58   305.4'2   81-13478
ISBN 0-674-44543-0 (cloth)   AACR2

ISBN 0-674-44544-9 (paper)

Acknowledgments

In acknowledging the generosity of others and the contributions
they have made to this work, I begin with the women, men, and
children who participated in the research I report. Their thoughtful-
ness in describing themselves and their lives, their patience in answering questions about morality, their willingness to discuss their
experiences of moral conflict and choice, are the foundation upon
which this book rests. I want to thank, in particular, the women
who participated in the abortion decision study; it was their hope
that their experience might be of help to others.

All of the research was a collaborative endeavor, and to my
collaborators I owe thanks as well—to Mary Belenky in the abortion decision study; to Michael Murphy in the college student
study; and to Michael Murphy, Sharry Langdale, and Nona Lyons
in the rights and responsibilities study. Many of the interviews were
conducted by them; many of the ideas arose in discussions we had.
The design of the studies reflects their contribution; the completion
of the research, their commitment and hard work. Michael
Basseches, Suzie Benack, Donna Hulsizer, Nancy Jacobs, Robert
Kegan, Deborah Lapidus, and Steven Ries also contributed in central ways to this work. Susan Pollak, my collaborator in the images
of violence study, made the observation which initiated that research.

The financial support that made this work possible came from
the Spencer Foundation which, through a grant to Harvard faculty,
provided funds for the abortion decision study; from The William

F. Milton Fund and the Small Grants Section of The National Institute for Mental Health (Grant # RO3MH31571), for the college student study; and from the National Institute of Education, for the rights and responsibilities study. A fellowship from the Mellon Foundation enabled me to spend a year at the Center for Research on Women at Wellesley College.

Support of another kind came from my colleagues at Harvard: from Lawrence Kohlberg who illuminated for me the study of morality and who has been, over many years, a good teacher and friend; from David McClelland and George Goethals who, also for many years, have inspired my work and been most generous in their encouragement: from Beatrice Whiting who expanded my vision; from William Perry whose research informed my own. I am grateful to Patricia Spacks and Stephanie Engel for collaborations in teaching that enlarged and clarified my perceptions; to Urie Bronfenbrenner, Matina Horner, Jane Lilienfeld, Malkah Notman, Barbara and Paul Rosenkrantz, and Dora Ullian for suggestions that expanded the scope of this work; to Janet Giele for her editorial inspiration; to Jane Martin for extensive comments on previous drafts; and to Virginia LaPlante for her many wise suggestions that improved the final manuscript.

Earlier versions of Chapters 1 and 3 appeared in the *Harvard Educational Review*, and my gratitude to the students on the editorial board for their careful attention and help. The Social Science Research Council kindly granted permission to reproduce portions of Chapter 6 that will appear, in different form, in a book sponsored by the Council and edited by Janet Giele.

To Eric Wanner of Harvard University Press, I am deeply indebted; it was he who sustained and informed my vision of this book. There were also some friends on whose help I particularly drew; for their willingness to listen and to read, for the generosity of their response, I thank Michael Murphy, Nona Lyons, Jean Baker Miller, and Christina Robb. To my sons, Jon, Tim, and Chris, I am grateful—for the pleasure of their interest and enthusiasm, for their ideas and perceptions, for their unflagging encouragement and support. And to my husband, Jim Gilligan, my thanks—for the insight of his ideas, for the clarity of his responses, for his help, his humor, and his perspective.

Contents

Introduction

OVER THE PAST TEN YEARS, I have been listening to people talking about morality and about themselves. Halfway through that time, I began to hear a distinction in these voices, two ways of speaking about moral problems, two modes of describing the relationship between other and self. Differences represented in the psychological literature as steps in a developmental progression suddenly appeared instead as a contrapuntal theme, woven into the cycle of life and recurring in varying forms in people's judgments, fantasies, and thoughts. The occasion for this observation was the selection of a sample of women for a study of the relation between judgment and action in a situation of moral conflict and choice. Against the background of the psychological descriptions of identity and moral development which I had read and taught for a number of years, the women's voices sounded distinct. It was then that I began to notice the recurrent problems in interpreting women's development and to connect these problems to the repeated exclusion of women from the critical theory-building studies of psychological research.

This book records different modes of thinking about relationships and the association of these modes with male and female voices in psychological and literary texts and in the data of my research. The disparity between women's experience and the representation of human development, noted throughout the psychological literature, has generally been seen to signify a problem in women's development. Instead, the failure of women to fit existing models of human growth may point to a problem in the representation, a limitation in the conception of human condition, an omission of certain truths about life.

The different voice I describe is characterized not by gender but theme. Its association with women is an empirical observation, and it is primarily through women's voices that I trace its development. But this association is not absolute, and the contrasts between male and female voices are presented here to highlight a distinction between two modes of thought and to focus a problem of interpretation rather than to represent a generalization about either sex. In tracing development, I point to the interplay of these voices within each sex and suggest that their convergence marks times of crisis and change. No claims are made about the origins of the differences described or their distribution in a wider population, across cultures, or through time. Clearly, these differences arise in a social context where factors of social status and power combine with reproductive biology to shape the experience of males and females and the relations between the sexes. My interest lies in the interaction of experience and thought, in different voices and the dialogues to which they give rise, in the way we listen to ourselves and to others, in the stories we tell about our lives.

Three studies are referred to throughout this book and reflect the central assumption of my research: that the way people talk about their lives is of significance, that the language they use and the connections they make reveal the world that they see and in which they act. All of the studies relied on interviews and included the same set of questions—about conceptions of self and morality, about experiences of conflict and choice. The method of interviewing was to follow the language and the logic of the person's thought, with the interviewer asking further questions in order to clarify the meaning of a particular response.

The *college student study* explored identity and moral development in the early adult years by relating the view of self and thinking about morality to experiences of moral conflict and the making of life choices. Twenty-five students, selected at random from a group who had chosen as sophomores to take a course on moral and political choice, were interviewed as seniors in college and then five years following graduation. In selecting this sample, I observed that of the twenty students who had dropped the course, sixteen were women. These women were also contacted and interviewed as seniors.

The *abortion decision study* considered the relation between experience and thought and the role of conflict in development. Twenty-nine women, ranging in age from fifteen to thirty-three, diverse in ethnic background and social class, some single, some married, a few the mother of a preschool child, were interviewed during the first trimester of a confirmed pregnancy at a time when they were considering abortion. These women were referred to the study through pregnancy counseling services and abortion clinics in a large metropolitan area; no effort was made to select a representative sample of the clinic or counseling service population. Of the twenty-nine women referred, complete interview data were available for twenty-four, and of these twenty-four, twenty-one were interviewed again at the end of the year following choice.

Both of these studies expanded the usual design of research on moral judgment by asking how people defined moral problems and what experiences they construed as moral conflicts in their lives, rather than by focusing on their thinking about problems presented to them for resolution. The hypotheses generated by these studies concerning different modes of thinking about morality and their relation to different views of self were further explored and refined through the *rights and responsibilities study*. This study involved a sample of males and females matched for age, intelligence, education, occupation, and social class at nine points across the life cycle: ages 6–9, 11, 15, 19, 22, 25–27, 35, 45, and 60. From a total sample of 144 (8 males and 8 females at each age), including a more intensively interviewed subsample of 36 (2 males and 2 females at each age), data were collected on conceptions of self and morality, experiences of moral conflict and choice, and judgments of hypothetical moral dilemmas.

In presenting excerpts from this work, I report research in progress whose aim is to provide, in the field of human development, a clearer representation of women's development which will enable psychologists and others to follow its course and understand some of the apparent puzzles it presents, especially those that pertain to women's identity formation and their moral development in adolescence and adulthood. For women, I hope this work will offer a representation of their thought that enables them to see better its integrity and validity, to recognize the experiences their thinking refracts, and to understand the line of its development. My goal is to expand the understanding of human development by using the group left out in the construction of theory to call attention to what is missing in its account. Seen in this light, the discrepant data on women's experience provide a basis upon which to generate new theory, potentially yielding a more encompassing view of the lives of both of the sexes.

1 Woman's Place in Man's Life Cycle

I N THE SECOND ACT of *The Cherry Orchard,* Lopahin, a young merchant, describes his life of hard work and success. Failing to convince Madame Ranevskaya to cut down the cherry orchard to save her estate, he will go on in the next act to buy it himself. He is the self-made man who, in purchasing the estate where his father and grandfather were slaves, seeks to eradicate the "awkward, unhappy life" of the past, replacing the cherry orchard with summer cottages where coming generations "will see a new life." In elaborating this developmental vision, he reveals the image of man that underlies and supports his activity: "At times when I can't go to sleep, I think: Lord, thou gavest us immense forests, unbounded fields and the widest horizons, and living in the midst of them we should indeed be giants"—at which point, Madame Ranevskaya interrupts him, saying, "You feel the need for giants—They are good only in fairy tales, anywhere else they only frighten us."

Conceptions of the human life cycle represent attempts to order and make coherent the unfolding experiences and perceptions, the changing wishes and realities of everyday life. But the nature of such conceptions depends in part on the position of the observer. The brief excerpt from Chekhov's play suggests that when the observer is a woman, the perspective may be of a different sort. Different judgments of the image of man as giant imply different ideas about human development, different ways of imagining the human condition, different notions of what is of value in life.

At a time when efforts are being made to eradicate discrimination between the sexes in the search for social equality and justice, the differences between the sexes are being rediscovered in the social sciences. This discovery occurs when theories formerly considered to be sexually neutral in their scientific objectivity are found instead to reflect a consistent observational and evaluative bias. Then the presumed neutrality of science, like that of language itself, gives way to the recognition that the categories of knowledge are human constructions. The fascination with point of view that has informed the fiction of the twentieth century and the corresponding recognition of the relativity of judgment infuse our scientific understanding as well when we begin to notice how accustomed we have become to seeing life through men's eyes.

A recent discovery of this sort pertains to the apparently innocent classic *The Elements of Style* by William Strunk and E. B. White. The Supreme Court ruling on the subject of discrimination in classroom texts led one teacher of English to notice that the elementary rules of English usage were being taught through examples which counterposed the birth of Napoleon, the writings of Coleridge, and statements such as "He was an interesting talker. A man who had traveled all over the world and lived in half a dozen countries," with "Well, Susan, this is a fine mess you are in" or, less drastically, "He saw a woman, accompanied by two children, walking slowly down the road."

Psychological theorists have fallen as innocently as Strunk and White into the same observational bias. Implicitly adopting the male life as the norm, they have tried to fashion women out of a masculine cloth. It all goes back, of course, to Adam and Eve—a story which shows, among other things, that if you make a woman out of a man, you are bound to get into trouble. In the life cycle, as in the Garden of Eden, the woman has been the deviant.

The penchant of developmental theorists to project a masculine image, and one that appears frightening to women, goes back at least to Freud (1905), who built his theory of psychosexual development around the experiences of the male child that culminate in the Oedipus complex. In the 1920s, Freud struggled to resolve the contradictions posed for his theory by the differences in female anatomy and the different configuration of the young girl's early family relationships. After trying to fit women into his masculine conception, seeing them as envying that which they missed, he came instead to acknowledge, in the strength and persistence of women's pre-Oedipal attachments to their mothers, a developmental difference. He considered this difference in women's development to be responsible for what he saw as women's developmental failure.

Having tied the formation of the superego or conscience to castration anxiety, Freud considered women to be deprived by nature of the impetus for a clear-cut Oedipal resolution. Consequently, women's superego—the heir to the Oedipus complex—was compromised: it was never "so inexorable, so impersonal, so independent of its emotional origins as we require it to be in men." From this observation of difference, that "for women the level of what is ethically normal is different from what it is in men," Freud concluded that women "show less sense of justice than men, that they are less ready to submit to the great exigencies of life, that they are more often influenced in their judgements by feelings of affection or hostility" (1925, pp. 257–258).

Thus a problem in theory became cast as a problem in women's development, and the problem in women's development was located in their experience of relationships. Nancy Chodorow (1974), attempting to account for "the reproduction within each generation of certain general and nearly universal differences that characterize masculine and feminine personality and roles," attributes these differences between the sexes not to anatomy but rather to "the fact that women, universally, are largely responsible for early child care." Because this early social environment differs for and is experienced differently by male and female children, basic sex differences recur in personality development. As a result, "in any given society, feminine personality comes to define itself in relation and connection to other people more than masculine personality does" (pp. 43–44).

In her analysis, Chodorow relies primarily on Robert Stoller's studies which indicate that gender identity, the unchanging core of personality formation, is "with rare exception firmly and irreversibly established for both sexes by the time a child is around three." Given that for both sexes the primary caretaker in the first three years of life is typically female, the interpersonal dynamics of gender identity formation are different for boys and girls. Female identity formation takes place in a context of ongoing relationship since "mothers tend to experience their daughters as more like, and continuous with, themselves." Correspondingly, girls, in identifying themselves as female, experience themselves as like their mothers, thus fusing the experience of attachment with the process of identity formation. In contrast, "mothers experience their sons as a male opposite," and boys, in defining themselves as masculine, separate their mothers from themselves, thus curtailing "their primary love and sense of empathic tie." Consequently, male development entails a "more emphatic individuation and a more defensive firming of experienced ego boundaries." For boys, but not girls, "issues of differentiation have become intertwined with sexual issues" (1978, pp. 150, 166–167).

Writing against the masculine bias of psychoanalytic theory, Chodorow argues that the existence of sex differences in the early experiences of individuation and relationship "does not mean that women have 'weaker' ego boundaries than men or are more prone to psychosis." It means instead that "girls emerge from this period with a basis for 'empathy' built into their primary definition of self in a way that boys do not." Chodorow thus replaces Freud's negative and derivative description of female psychology with a positive and direct account of her own: "Girls emerge with a stronger basis for experiencing another's needs or feelings as one's own (or of thinking that one is so experiencing another's needs and feelings). Furthermore, girls do not define themselves in terms of the denial of preoedipal relational modes to the same extent as do boys. Therefore, regression to these modes tends not to feel as much a basic threat to their ego. From very early, then, because they are parented by a person of the same gender ... girls come to experience themselves as less differentiated than boys, as more continuous with and related to the external object-world, and as differently oriented to their inner object-world as well" (p. 167).

Consequently, relationships, and particularly issues of dependency, are experienced differently by women and men. For boys and men, separation and individuation are critically tied to gender identity since separation from the mother is essential for the development of masculinity. For girls and women, issues of femininity or feminine identity do not depend on the achievement of separation from the mother or on the progress of individuation. Since masculinity is defined through separation while femininity is defined through attachment, male gender identity is threatened by intimacy while female gender identity is threatened by separation. Thus males tend to have difficulty with relationships, while females tend to have problems with individuation. The quality of embeddedness in social interaction and personal relationships that characterizes women's lives in contrast to men's, however, becomes not only a descriptive difference but also a developmental liability when the milestones of childhood and adolescent development in the psychological literature are markers of increasing separation. Women's failure to separate then becomes by definition a failure to develop.

The sex differences in personality formation that Chodorow describes in early childhood appear during the middle childhood years in studies of children's games. Children's games are considered by George Herbert Mead (1934) and Jean Piaget (1932) as the crucible of social development during the school years. In games, children learn to take the role of the other and come to see themselves through another's eyes. In games, they learn respect for rules and come to understand the ways rules can be made and changed.

Janet Lever (1976), considering the peer group to be the agent of socialization during the elementary school years and play to be a major activity of socialization at that time, set out to discover whether there are sex differences in the games that children play. Studying 181 fifth-grade, white, middle-class children, ages ten and eleven, she observed the organization and structure of their playtime activities. She watched the children as they played at school during recess and in physical education class, and in addition kept diaries of their accounts as to how they spent their out-of-school time. From this study, Lever reports sex differences: boys play out of doors more often than girls do; boys play more often in large and age-heterogeneous groups; they play competitive games more often, and their games last longer than girls' games. The last is in some ways the most interesting finding. Boys' games appeared to last longer not only because they required a higher level of skill and were thus less likely to become boring, but also because, when disputes arose in the course of a game, boys were able to resolve the disputes more effectively than girls: "During the course of this study, boys were seen quarrelling all the time, but not once was a game terminated because of a quarrel and no game was interrupted for more than seven minutes. In the gravest debates, the final word was always, to 'repeat the play,' generally followed by a chorus of 'cheater's proof' " (p. 482). In fact, it seemed that the boys enjoyed the legal debates as much as they did the game itself, and even marginal players of lesser size or skill participated equally in these recurrent squabbles. In contrast, the eruption of disputes among girls tended to end the game.

Thus Lever extends and corroborates the observations of Piaget in his study of the rules of the game, where he finds boys becoming through childhood increasingly fascinated with the legal elaboration of rules and the development of fair procedures for adjudicating conflicts, a fascination that, he notes, does not hold for girls. Girls, Piaget observes, have a more "pragmatic" attitude toward rules, "regarding a rule as good as long as the game repaid it" (p. 83). Girls are more tolerant in their attitudes toward rules, more willing to make exceptions, and more easily reconciled to innovations. As a result, the legal sense, which Piaget considers essential to moral development, "is far less developed in little girls than in boys" (p.77).

The bias that leads Piaget to equate male development with child development also colors Lever's work. The assumption that shapes her discussion of results is that the male model is the better one since it fits the requirements for modern corporate success. In contrast, the sensitivity and care for the feelings of others that girls develop through their play have little market value and can even impede professional success. Lever implies that, given the realities of adult life, if a girl does not want to be left dependent on men, she will have to learn to play like a boy.

To Piaget's argument that children learn the respect for rules necessary for moral development by playing rule-bound games, Lawrence Kohlberg (1969) adds that these lessons are most effectively learned through the opportunities for role-taking that arise in the course of resolving disputes. Consequently, the moral lessons inherent in girls' play appear to be fewer than in boys'. Traditional girls' games like jump rope and hopscotch are turn-taking games, where competition is indirect since one person's success does not necessarily signify another's failure. Consequently, disputes requiring adjudication are less likely to occur. In fact, most of the girls whom Lever interviewed claimed that when a quarrel broke out, they ended the game. Rather than elaborating a system of rules for resolving disputes, girls subordinated the continuation of the game to the continuation of relationships.

Lever concludes that from the games they play, boys learn both the independence and the organizational skills necessary for coordinating the activities of large and diverse groups of people. By participating in controlled and socially approved competitive situations, they learn to deal with competition in a relatively forthright manner—to play with their enemies and to compete with their friends—all in accordance with the rules of the game. In contrast, girls' play tends to occur in smaller, more intimate groups, often the best-friend dyad, and in private places. This play replicates the social pattern of primary human relationships in that its organization is more cooperative. Thus, it points less, in Mead's terms, toward learning to take the role of "the generalized other," less toward the abstraction of human relationships. But it fosters the development of the empathy and sensitivity necessary for taking the role of "the particular other" and points more toward knowing the other as different from the self.

The sex differences in personality formation in early childhood that Chodorow derives from her analysis of the mother-child relationship are thus extended by Lever's observations of sex differences in the play activities of middle childhood. Together these accounts suggest that boys and girls arrive at puberty with a different interpersonal orientation and a different range of social experiences. Yet, since adolescence is considered a crucial time for separation, the period of "the second individuation process" (Blos, 1967), female development has appeared most divergent and thus most problematic at this time.

"Puberty," Freud says, "which brings about so great an accession of libido in boys, is marked in girls by a fresh wave of *repression*," necessary for the transformation of the young girl's "masculine sexuality" into the specifically feminine sexuality of her adulthood (1905, pp. 220–221). Freud posits this transformation on the girl's acknowledgment and acceptance of "the fact of her castration" (1931, p. 229). To the girl, Freud explains, puberty brings a new awareness of "the wound to her narcissism" and leads her to develop, "like a scar, a sense of inferiority"(1925, p. 253). Since in Erik Erikson's expansion of Freud's psychoanalytic account, adolescence is the time when development hinges on identity, the girl arrives at this juncture either psychologically at risk or with a different agenda.

The problem that female adolescence presents for theorists of human development is apparent in Erikson's scheme. Erikson (1950) charts eight stages of psychosocial development, of which adolescence is the fifth. The task at this stage is to forge a coherent sense of self, to verify an identity that can span the discontinuity of puberty and make possible the adult capacity to love and work. The preparation for the successful resolution of the adolescent identity crisis is delineated in Erikson's description of the crises that characterize the preceding four stages. Although the initial crisis in infancy of "trust versus mistrust" anchors development in the experience of relationship, the task then clearly becomes one of individuation. Erikson's second stage centers on the crisis of "autonomy versus shame and doubt," which marks the walking child's emerging sense of separateness and agency. From there, development goes on through the crisis of "initiative versus guilt," successful resolution of which represents a further move in the direction of autonomy. Next, following the inevitable disappointment of the magical wishes of the Oedipal period, children realize that to compete with their parents, they must first join them and learn to do what they do so well. Thus in the middle childhood years, development turns on the crisis of "industry versus inferiority," as the demonstration of competence becomes critical to the child's developing self-esteem. This is the time when children strive to learn and master the technology of their culture, in order to recognize themselves and to be recognized by others as capable of becoming adults. Next comes adolescence, the celebration of the autonomous, initiating, industrious self through the forging of an identity based on an ideology that can support and justify adult commitments. But about whom is Erikson talking?

Once again it turns out to be the male child. For the female, Erikson (1968) says, the sequence is a bit different. She holds her identity in abeyance as she prepares to attract the man by whose name she will be known, by whose status she will be defined, the man who will rescue her from emptiness and loneliness by filling "the inner space." While for men, identity precedes intimacy and generativity in the optimal cycle of human separation and attachment, for women these tasks seem instead to be fused. Intimacy goes along with identity, as the female comes to know herself as she is known, through her relationships with others.

Yet despite Erikson's observation of sex differences, his chart of life-cycle stages remains unchanged: identity continues to precede intimacy as male experience continues to define his life-cycle conception. But in this male life cycle there is little preparation for the intimacy of the first adult stage. Only the initial stage of trust versus mistrust suggests the type of mutuality that Erikson means by intimacy and generativity and Freud means by genitality. The rest is separateness, with the result that development itself comes to be identified with separation, and attachments appear to be developmental impediments, as is repeatedly the case in the assessment of women.

Erikson's description of male identity as forged in relation to the world and of female identity as awakened in a relationship of intimacy with another person is hardly new. In the fairy tales that Bruno Bettelheim (1976) describes an identical portrayal appears. The dynamics of male adolescence are illustrated archetypically by the conflict between father and son in "The Three Languages." Here a son, considered hopelessly stupid by his father, is given one last chance at education and sent for a year to study with a master. But when he returns, all he has learned is "what the dogs bark." After two further attempts of this sort, the father gives up in disgust and orders his servants to take the child into the forest and kill him. But the servants, those perpetual rescuers of disowned and abandoned children, take pity on the child and decide simply to leave him in the forest. From there, his wanderings take him to a land beset by furious dogs whose barking permits nobody to rest and who periodically devour one of the inhabitants. Now it turns out that our hero has learned just the right thing: he can talk with the dogs and is able to quiet them, thus restoring peace to the land. Since the other knowledge he acquires serves him equally well, he emerges triumphant from his adolescent confrontation with his father, a giant of the life-cycle conception.

In contrast, the dynamics of female adolescence are depicted through the telling of a very different story. In the world of the fairy tale, the girl's first bleeding is followed by a period of intense passivity in which nothing seems to be happening. Yet in the deep sleeps of Snow White and Sleeping Beauty, Bettelheim sees that inner concentration which he considers to be the necessary counterpart to the activity of adventure. Since the adolescent heroines awake from their sleep, not to conquer the world, but to marry the prince, their identity is inwardly and interpersonally defined. For women, in Bettelheim's as in Erikson's account, identity and intimacy are intricately conjoined. The sex differences depicted in the world of fairy tales, like the fantasy of the woman warrior in Maxine Hong Kingston's (1977) recent autobiographical novel which echoes the old stories of Troilus and Cressida and Tancred and Chlorinda, indicate repeatedly that active adventure is a male activity, and that if a woman is to embark on such endeavors, she must at least dress like a man.

These observations about sex difference support the conclusion reached by David McClelland (1975) that "sex role turns out to be one of the most important determinants of human behavior; psychologists have found sex differences in their studies from the moment they started doing empirical research." But since it is difficult to say "different" without saying "better" or "worse," since there is a tendency to construct a single scale of measurement, and since that scale has generally been derived from and standardized on the basis of men's interpretations of research data drawn predominantly or exclusively from studies of males, psychologists "have tended to regard male behavior as the 'norm' and female behavior as some kind of deviation from that norm" (p. 81). Thus, when women do not conform to the standards of psychological expectation, the conclusion has generally been that something is wrong with the women.

What Matina Horner (1972) found to be wrong with women was the anxiety they showed about competitive achievement. From the beginning, research on human motivation using the Thematic Apperception Test (TAT) was plagued by evidence of sex differences which appeared to confuse and complicate data analysis. The TAT presents for interpretation an ambiguous cue—a picture about which a story is to be written or a segment of a story that is to be completed. Such stories, in reflecting projective imagination, are considered by psychologists to reveal the ways in which people construe what they perceive, that is, the concepts and interpretations they bring to their experience and thus presumably the kind of sense that they make of their lives. Prior to Horner's work it was clear that women made a different kind of sense than men of situations of competitive achievement, that in some way they saw the situations differently or the situations aroused in them some different response.

On the basis of his studies of men, McClelland divided the concept of achievement motivation into what appeared to be its two logical components, a motive to approach success ("hope success") and a motive to avoid failure ("fear failure"). From her studies of women, Horner identified as a third category the unlikely motivation to avoid success ("fear success"). Women appeared to have a problem with competitive achievement, and that problem seemed to emanate from a perceived conflict between femininity and success, the dilemma of the female adolescent who struggles to integrate her feminine aspirations and the identifications of her early childhood with the more masculine competence she has acquired at school. From her analysis of women's completions of a story that began, "after first term finals, Anne finds herself at the top of her medical school class," and from her observation of women's performance in competitive achievement situations, Horner reports that, "when success is likely or possible, threatened by the negative consequences they expect to follow success, young women become anxious and their positive achievement strivings become thwarted" (p. 171). She concludes that this fear "exists because for most women, the anticipation of success in competitive achievement activity, especially against men, produces anticipation of certain negative consequences, for example, threat of social rejection and loss of femininity" (1968, p. 125).

Such conflicts about success, however, may be viewed in a different light. Georgia Sassen (1980) suggests that the conflicts expressed by the women might instead indicate "a heightened perception of the 'other side' of competitive success, that is, the great emotional costs at which success achieved through competition is often gained—an understanding which, though confused, indicates some underlying sense that something is rotten in the state in which success is defined as having better grades than everyone else" (p. 15). Sassen points out that Horner found success anxiety to be present in women only when achievement was directly competitive, that is, when one person's success was at the expense of another's failure.

In his elaboration of the identity crisis, Erikson (1968) cites the life of George Bernard Shaw to illustrate the young person's sense of being co-opted prematurely by success in a career he cannot wholeheartedly endorse. Shaw at seventy, reflecting upon his life, described his crisis at the age of twenty as having been caused not by the lack of success or the absence of recognition, but by too much of both: "I made good in spite of myself, and found, to my dismay, that Business, instead of expelling me as the worthless imposter I was, was fastening upon me with no intention of letting me go. Behold me, therefore, in my twentieth year, with a business training, in an occupation which I detested as cordially as any sane person lets himself detest anything he cannot escape from. In March 1876 I broke loose" (p. 143). At this point Shaw settled down to study and write as he pleased. Hardly interpreted as evidence of neurotic anxiety about achievement and competition, Shaw's refusal suggests to Erikson "the extraordinary workings of an extraordinary personality [coming] to the fore" (p. 144).

We might on these grounds begin to ask, not why women have conflicts about competitive success, but why men show such readiness to adopt and celebrate a rather narrow vision of success. Remembering Piaget's observation, corroborated by Lever, that boys in their games are more concerned with rules while girls are more concerned with relationships, often at the expense of the game itself—and given Chodorow's conclusion that men's social orientation is positional while women's is personal—we begin to understand why, when "Anne" becomes "John" in Horner's tale of competitive success and the story is completed by men, fear of success tends to disappear. John is considered to have played by the rules and won. He has the *right* to feel good about his success. Confirmed in the sense of his own identity as separate from those who, compared to him, are less competent, his positional sense of self is affirmed. For Anne, it is possible that the position she could obtain by being at the top of her medical school class may not, in fact, be what she wants.

"It is obvious," Virginia Woolf says, "that the values of women differ very often from the values which have been made by the other sex" (1929, p. 76). Yet, she adds, "it is the masculine values that prevail." As a result, women come to question the normality of their feelings and to alter their judgments in deference to the opinion of others. In the nineteenth century novels written by women, Woolf sees at work "a mind which was slightly pulled from the straight and made to alter its clear vision in deference to external authority." The same deference to the values and opinions of others can be seen in the judgments of twentieth century women. The difficulty women experience in finding or speaking publicly in their own voices emerges repeatedly in the form of qualification and self-doubt, but also in intimations of a divided judgment, a public assessment and private assessment which are fundamentally at odds.

Yet the deference and confusion that Woolf criticizes in women derive from the values she sees as their strength. Women's deference is rooted not only in their social subordination but also in the substance of their moral concern. Sensitivity to the needs of others and the assumption of responsibility for taking care lead women to attend to voices other than their own and to include in their judgment other points of view. Women's moral weakness, manifest in an apparent diffusion and confusion of judgment, is thus inseparable from women's moral strength, an overriding concern with relationships and responsibilities. The reluctance to judge may itself be indicative of the care and concern for others that infuse the psychology of women's development and are responsible for what is generally seen as problematic in its nature.

Thus women not only define themselves in a context of human relationship but also judge themselves in terms of their ability to care. Women's place in man's life cycle has been that of nurturer, caretaker, and helpmate, the weaver of those networks of relationships on which she in turn relies. But while women have thus taken care of men, men have, in their theories of psychological development, as in their economic arrangements, tended to assume or devalue that care. When the focus on individuation and individual achievement extends into adulthood and maturity is equated with personal autonomy, concern with relationships appears as a weakness of women rather than as a human strength (Miller, 1976).

The discrepancy between womanhood and adulthood is nowhere more evident than in the studies on sex-role stereotypes reported by Broverman, Vogel, Broverman, Clarkson, and Rosenkrantz (1972). The repeated finding of these studies is that the qualities deemed necessary for adulthood—the capacity for autonomous thinking, clear decision-making, and responsible action—are those associated with masculinity and considered undesirable as attributes of the feminine self. The stereotypes suggest a splitting of love and work that relegates expressive capacities to women while placing instrumental abilities in the masculine domain. Yet looked at from a different perspective, these stereotypes reflect a conception of adulthood that is itself out of balance, favoring the separateness of the individual self over connection to others, and leaning more toward an autonomous life of work than toward the interdependence of love and care.

The discovery now being celebrated by men in mid-life of the importance of intimacy, relationships, and care is something that women have known from the beginning. However, because that knowledge in women has been considered "intuitive" or "instinctive," a function of anatomy coupled with destiny, psychologists have neglected to describe its development. In my research, I have found that women's moral development centers on the elaboration of that knowledge and thus delineates a critical line of psychological development in the lives of both of the sexes. The subject of moral development not only provides the final illustration of the reiterative pattern in the observation and assessment of sex differences in the literature on human development, but also indicates more particularly why the nature and significance of women's development has been for so long obscured and shrouded in mystery.

The criticism that Freud makes of women's sense of justice, seeing it as compromised in its refusal of blind impartiality, reappears not only in the work of Piaget but also in that of Kohlberg. While in Piaget's account (1932) of the moral judgment of the child, girls are an aside, a curiosity to whom he devotes four brief entries in an index that omits "boys" altogether because "the child" is assumed to be male, in the research from which Kohlberg derives his theory, females simply do not exist. Kohlberg's (1958, 1981) six stages that describe the development of moral judgment from childhood to adulthood are based empirically on a study of eighty-four boys whose development Kohlberg has followed for a period of over twenty years. Although Kohlberg claims universality for his stage sequence, those groups not included in his original sample rarely reach his higher stages (Edwards, 1975; Holstein, 1976; Simpson, 1974). Prominent among those who thus appear to be deficient in moral development when measured by Kohlberg's scale are women, whose judgments seem to exemplify the third stage of his six-stage sequence. At this stage morality is conceived in interpersonal terms and goodness is equated with helping and pleasing others. This conception of goodness is considered by Kohlberg and Kramer (1969) to be functional in the lives of mature women insofar as their lives take place in the home. Kohlberg and Kramer imply that only if women enter the traditional arena of male activity will they recognize the inadequacy of this moral perspective and progress like men toward higher stages where relationships are subordinated to rules (stage four) and rules to universal principles of justice (stages five and six).

Yet herein lies a paradox, for the very traits that traditionally have defined the "goodness" of women, their care for and sensitivity to the needs of others, are those that mark them as deficient in moral development. In this version of moral development, however, the conception of maturity is derived from the study of men's lives and reflects the importance of individuation in their development. Piaget (1970), challenging the common impression that a developmental theory is built like a pyramid from its base in infancy, points out that a conception of development instead hangs from its vertex of maturity, the point toward which progress is traced. Thus, a change in the definition of maturity does not simply alter the description of the highest stage but recasts the understanding of development, changing the entire account.

When one begins with the study of women and derives developmental constructs from their lives, the outline of a moral conception different from that described by Freud, Piaget, or Kohlberg begins to emerge and informs a different description of development. In this conception, the moral problem arises from conflicting responsibilities rather than from competing rights and requires for its resolution a mode of thinking that is contextual and narrative rather than formal and abstract. This conception of morality as concerned with the activity of care centers moral development around the understanding of responsibility and relationships, just as the conception of morality as fairness ties moral development to the understanding of rights and rules.

This different construction of the moral problem by women may be seen as the critical reason for their failure to develop within the constraints of Kohlberg's system. Regarding all constructions of responsibility as evidence of a conventional moral understanding, Kohlberg defines the highest stages of moral development as deriving from a reflective understanding of human rights. That the morality of rights differs from the morality of responsibility in its emphasis on separation rather than connection, in its consideration of the individual rather than the relationship as primary, is illustrated by two responses to interview questions about the nature of morality. The first comes from a twenty-five-year-old man, one of the participants in Kohlberg's study:

> [*What does the word morality mean to you?*] Nobody in the world knows the answer. I think it is recognizing the right of the individual, the rights of other individuals, not interfering with those rights. Act as fairly as you would have them treat you. I think it is basically to preserve the human being's right to existence. I think that is the most important. Secondly, the human being's right to do as he pleases, again without interfering with somebody else's rights.
>
> [*How have your views on morality changed since the last interview?*] I think I am more aware of an individual's rights now. I used to be looking at it strictly from my point of view, just for me. Now I think I am more aware of what the individual has a right to.

Kohlberg (1973) cites this man's response as illustrative of the principled conception of human rights that exemplifies his fifth and sixth stages. Commenting on the response, Kohlberg says: "Moving to a perspective outside of that of his society, he identifies morality with justice (fairness, rights, the Golden Rule), with recognition of the rights of others as these are defined naturally or intrinscially. The human's being right to do as he pleases without interfering with somebody else's rights is a formula defining rights prior to social legislation" (pp. 29–30).

The second response comes from a woman who participated in the rights and responsibilities study. She also was twenty-five and, at the time, a third-year law student:

> [*Is there really some correct solution to moral problems, or is everybody's opinion equally right?*] No, I don't think everybody's opinion is equally right. I think that in some situations there may be opinions that are equally valid, and one could conscientiously adopt one of several courses of action. But there are other situations in which I think there are right and wrong answers, that sort of inhere in the nature of existence, of all individuals here who need to live with each other to live. We need to depend on each other, and hopefully it is not only a physical need but a need of fulfillment in ourselves, that a person's life is enriched by cooperating with other people and striving to live in harmony with everybody else, and to that end, there are right and wrong, there are things which promote that end and that move away from it, and in that way it is possible to choose in certain cases among different courses of action that obviously promote or harm that goal.
>
> [*Is there a time in the past when you would have thought about these things differently?*] Oh, yeah, I think that I went through a time when I thought that things were pretty relative, that I can't tell you what to do and you can't tell me what to do, because you've got your conscience and I've got mine.
>
> [*When was that?*] When I was in high school. I guess that it just sort of dawned on me that my own ideas changed, and because my own judgment changed, I felt I couldn't judge another person's judgment. But now I think even when it is only the person himself who is going to be affected, I say it is wrong to the extent it doesn't cohere with what I know about human nature and what I know about you, and just from

what I think is true about the operation of the universe, I could say I think you are making a mistake.

[*What led you to change, do you think?*] Just seeing more of life, just recognizing that there are an awful lot of things that are common among people. There are certain things that you come to learn promote a better life and better relationships and more personal fulfillment than other things that in general tend to do the opposite, and the things that promote these things, you would call morally right.

This response also represents a personal reconstruction of morality following a period of questioning and doubt, but the reconstruction of moral understanding is based not on the primacy and universality of individual rights, but rather on what she describes as a "very strong sense of being responsible to the world." Within this construction, the moral dilemma changes from how to exercise one's rights without interfering with the rights of others to how "to lead a moral life which includes obligations to myself and my family and people in general." The problem then becomes one of limiting responsibilities without abandoning moral concern. When asked to describe herself, this woman says that she values "having other people that I am tied to, and also having people that I am responsible to. I have a very strong sense of being responsible to the world, that I can't just live for my enjoyment, but just the fact of being in the world gives me an obligation to do what I can to make the world a better place to live in, no matter how small a scale that may be on." Thus while Kohlberg's subject worries about people interfering with each other's rights, this woman worries about "the possibility of omission, of your not helping others when you could help them."

The issue that this woman raises is addressed by Jane Loevinger's fifth "autonomous" stage of ego development, where autonomy, placed in a context of relationships, is defined as modulating an excessive sense of responsibility through the recognition that other people have responsibility for their own destiny. The autonomous stage in Loevinger's account (1970) witnesses a relinquishing of moral dichotomies and their replacement with "a feeling for the complexity and multifaceted character of real people and real situations" (p. 6). Whereas the rights conception of morality that informs Kohlberg's principled level (stages five and six) is geared to arriving at an objectively fair or just resolution to moral dilemmas

upon which all rational persons could agree, the responsibility conception focuses instead on the limitations of any particular resolution and describes the conflicts that remain.

Thus it becomes clear why a morality of rights and noninterference may appear frightening to women in its potential justification of indifference and unconcern. At the same time, it becomes
clear why, from a male perspective, a morality of responsibility appears inconclusive and diffuse, given its insistent contextual relativism. Women's moral judgments thus elucidate the pattern observed
in the description of the developmental differences between the
sexes, but they also provide an alternative conception of maturity
by which these differences can be assessed and their implications
traced. The psychology of women that has consistently been described as distinctive in its greater orientation toward relationships
and interdependence implies a more contextual mode of judgment
and a different moral understanding. Given the differences in
women's conceptions of self and morality, women bring to the life
cycle a different point of view and order human experience in terms
of different priorities.

The myth of Demeter and Persephone, which McClelland
(1975) cites as exemplifying the feminine attitude toward power,
was associated with the Eleusinian Mysteries celebrated in ancient
Greece for over two thousand years. As told in the Homeric *Hymn
to Demeter,* the story of Persephone indicates the strengths of interdependence, building up resources and giving, that McClelland
found in his research on power motivation to characterize the mature feminine style. Although, McClelland says, "it is fashionable to
conclude that no one knows what went on in the Mysteries, it is
known that they were probably the most important religious cere-
monies, even partly on the historical record, which were organized
by and for women, especially at the onset before men by means of
the cult of Dionysos began to take them over." Thus McClelland
regards the myth as "a special presentation of feminine psychology" (p. 96). It is, as well, a life-cycle story par excellence.

Persephone, the daughter of Demeter, while playing in a
meadow with her girlfriends, sees a beautiful narcissus which she
runs to pick. As she does so, the earth opens and she is snatched
away by Hades, who takes her to his underworld kingdom. Demeter, goddess of the earth, so mourns the loss of her daughter that
she refuses to allow anything to grow. The crops that sustain life on
earth shrivel up, killing men and animals alike, until Zeus takes

pity on man's suffering and persuades his brother to return Persephone to her mother. But before she leaves, Persephone eats some pomegranate seeds, which ensures that she will spend part of every year with Hades in the underworld.

The elusive mystery of women's development lies in its recognition of the continuing importance of attachment in the human life cycle. Woman's place in man's life cycle is to protect this recognition while the developmental litany intones the celebration of separation, autonomy, individuation, and natural rights. The myth of Persephone speaks directly to the distortion in this view by reminding us that narcissism leads to death, that the fertility of the earth is in some mysterious way tied to the continuation of the mother-daughter relationship, and that the life cycle itself arises from an alternation between the world of women and that of men. Only when life-cycle theorists divide their attention and begin to live with women as they have lived with men will their vision encompass the experience of both sexes and their theories become correspondingly more fertile.

2 Images
of
Relationship

N 1914, with his essay "On Narcissism," Freud swallows his distaste at the thought of "abandoning observation for barren theoretical controversy" and extends his map of the psychological domain. Tracing the development of the capacity to love, which he equates with maturity and psychic health, he locates its origins in the contrast between love for the mother and love for the self. But in thus dividing the world of love into narcissism and "object" relationships, he finds that while men's development becomes clearer, women's becomes increasingly opaque. The problem arises because the contrast between mother and self yields two different images of relationships. Relying on the imagery of men's lives in charting the course of human growth, Freud is unable to trace in women the development of relationships, morality, or a clear sense of self. This difficulty in fitting the logic of his theory to women's experience leads him in the end to set women apart, marking their relationships, like their sexual life, as "a 'dark continent' for psychology" (1926, p. 212).

Thus the problem of interpretation that shadows the understanding of women's development arises from the differences observed in their experience of relationships. To Freud, though living surrounded by women and otherwise seeing so much and so well, women's relationships seemed increasingly mysterious, difficult to discern, and hard to describe. While this mystery indicates how theory can blind observation, it also suggests that development in women is masked by a particular conception of human relationships. Since the imagery of relationships shapes the narrative of human development, the inclusion of women, by changing that imagery, implies a change in the entire account.

The shift in imagery that creates the problem in interpreting women's development is elucidated by the moral judgments of two eleven-year-old children, a boy and a girl, who see, in the same dilemma, two very different moral problems. While current theory brightly illuminates the line and the logic of the boy's thought, it casts scant light on that of the girl. The choice of a girl whose moral judgments elude existing categories of developmental assessment is meant to highlight the issue of interpretation rather than to exemplify sex differences per se. Adding a new line of interpretation, based on the imagery of the girl's thought, makes it possible not only to see development where previously development was not discerned but also to consider differences in the understanding of relationships without scaling these differences from better to worse.

The two children were in the same sixth-grade class at school and were participants in the rights and responsibilities study, designed to explore different conceptions of morality and self. The sample selected for this study was chosen to focus the variables of gender and age while maximizing developmental potential by holding constant, at a high level, the factors of intelligence, education, and social class that have been associated with moral development, at least as measured by existing scales. The two children in question, Amy and Jake, were both bright and articulate and, at least in their eleven-year-old aspirations, resisted easy categories of sex-role stereotyping, since Amy aspired to become a scientist while Jake preferred English to math. Yet their moral judgments seem initially to confirm familiar notions about differences between the sexes, suggesting that the edge girls have on moral development during the early school years gives way at puberty with the ascendance of formal logical thought in boys.

The dilemma that these eleven-year-olds were asked to resolve was one in the series devised by Kohlberg to measure moral development in adolescence by presenting a conflict between moral norms and exploring the logic of its resolution. In this particular dilemma, a man named Heinz considers whether or not to steal a drug which he cannot afford to buy in order to save the life of his wife. In the standard format of Kohlberg's interviewing procedure,

the description of the dilemma itself—Heinz's predicament, the
wife's disease, the druggist's refusal to lower his price—is followed
by the question, "Should Heinz steal the drug?" The reasons for
and against stealing are then explored through a series of questions
that vary and extend the parameters of the dilemma in a way designed to reveal the underlying structure of moral thought.

Jake, at eleven, is clear from the outset that Heinz should steal
the drug. Constructing the dilemma, as Kohlberg did, as a conflict
between the values of property and life, he discerns the logical priority of life and uses that logic to justify his choice:

> For one thing, a human life is worth more than money, and if
> the druggist only makes $1,000, he is still going to live, but if
> Heinz doesn't steal the drug, his wife is going to die. (*Why is
> life worth more than money?*) Because the druggist can get a
> thousand dollars later from rich people with cancer, but Heinz
> can't get his wife again. (*Why not?*) Because people are all dif-
> ferent and so you couldn't get Heinz's wife again.

Asked whether Heinz should steal the drug if he does not love his
wife, Jake replies that he should, saying that not only is there "a
difference between hating and killing," but also, if Heinz were
caught, "the judge would probably think it was the right thing to
do." Asked about the fact that, in stealing, Heinz would be breaking the law, he says that "the laws have mistakes, and you can't go
writing up a law for everything that you can imagine."

Thus, while taking the law into account and recognizing its
function in maintaining social order (the judge, Jake says, "should
give Heinz the lightest possible sentence"), he also sees the law as
man-made and therefore subject to error and change. Yet his judgment that Heinz should steal the drug, like his view of the law as
having mistakes, rests on the assumption of agreement, a societal
consensus around moral values that allows one to know and expect
others to recognize what is "the right thing to do."

Fascinated by the power of logic, this eleven-year-old boy locates truth in math, which, he says, is "the only thing that is totally
logical." Considering the moral dilemma to be "sort of like a math
problem with humans," he sets it up as an equation and proceeds
to work out the solution. Since his solution is rationally derived, he
assumes that anyone following reason would arrive at the same

conclusion and thus that a judge would also consider stealing to be the right thing for Heinz to do. Yet he is also aware of the limits of logic. Asked whether there is a right answer to moral problems, Jake replies that "there can only be right and wrong in judgment," since the parameters of action are variable and complex. Illustrating how actions undertaken with the best of intentions can eventuate in the most disastrous of consequences, he says, "like if you give an old lady your seat on the trolley, if you are in a trolley crash and that seat goes through the window, it might be that reason that the old lady dies."

Theories of developmental psychology illuminate well the position of this child, standing at the juncture of childhood and adolescence, at what Piaget describes as the pinnacle of childhood intelligence, and beginning through thought to discover a wider universe of possibility. The moment of preadolescence is caught by the conjunction of formal operational thought with a description of self still anchored in the factual parameters of his childhood world—his age, his town, his father's occupation, the substance of his likes, dislikes, and beliefs. Yet as his self-description radiates the self-confidence of a child who has arrived, in Erikson's terms, at a favorable balance of industry over inferiority—competent, sure of himself, and knowing well the rules of the game—so his emergent capacity for formal thought, his ability to think about thinking and to reason things out in a logical way, frees him from dependence on authority and allows him to find solutions to problems by himself.

This emergent autonomy follows the trajectory that Kohlberg's six stages of moral development trace, a three-level progression from an egocentric understanding of fairness based on individual need (stages one and two), to a conception of fairness anchored in the shared conventions of societal agreement (stages three and four), and finally to a principled understanding of fairness that rests on the free-standing logic of equality and reciprocity (stages five and six). While this boy's judgments at eleven are scored as conventional on Kohlberg's scale, a mixture of stages three and four, his ability to bring deductive logic to bear on the solution of moral dilemmas, to differentiate morality from law, and to see how laws can be considered to have mistakes points toward the principled conception of justice that Kohlberg equates with moral maturity.

In contrast, Amy's response to the dilemma conveys a very

different impression, an image of development stunted by a failure of logic, an inability to think for herself. Asked if Heinz should steal the drug, she replies in a way that seems evasive and unsure:

> Well, I don't think so. I think there might be other ways besides stealing it, like if he could borrow the money or make a loan or something, but he really shouldn't steal the drug—but his wife shouldn't die either.

Asked why he should not steal the drug, she considers neither property nor law but rather the effect that theft could have on the relationship between Heinz and his wife:

> If he stole the drug, he might save his wife then, but if he did, he might have to go to jail, and then his wife might get sicker again, and he couldn't get more of the drug, and it might not be good. So, they should really just talk it out and find some other way to make the money.

Seeing in the dilemma not a math problem with humans but a narrative of relationships that extends over time, Amy envisions the wife's continuing need for her husband and the husband's continuing concern for his wife and seeks to respond to the druggist's need in a way that would sustain rather than sever connection. Just as she ties the wife's survival to the preservation of relationships, so she considers the value of the wife's life in a context of relationships, saying that it would be wrong to let her die because, "if she died, it hurts a lot of people and it hurts her." Since Amy's moral judgment is grounded in the belief that, "if somebody has something that would keep somebody alive, then it's not right not to give it to them," she considers the problem in the dilemma to arise not from the druggist's assertion of rights but from his failure of response.

As the interviewer proceeds with the series of questions that follow from Kohlberg's construction of the dilemma, Amy's answers remain essentially unchanged, the various probes serving neither to elucidate nor to modify her initial response. Whether or not Heinz loves his wife, he still shouldn't steal or let her die; if it were a stranger dying instead, Amy says that "if the stranger didn't have anybody near or anyone she knew," then Heinz should try to save her life, but he should not steal the drug. But as the interviewer conveys through the repetition of questions that the answers she gave were not heard or not right, Amy's confidence begins to diminish, and her replies become more constrained and unsure. Asked again why Heinz should not steal the drug, she simply repeats, "Because it's not right." Asked again to explain why, she states again that theft would not be a good solution, adding lamely, "if he took it, he might not know how to give it to his wife, and so his wife might still die." Failing to see the dilemma as a self-contained problem in moral logic, she does not discern the internal structure of its resolution; as she constructs the problem differently herself, Kohlberg's conception completely evades her.

Instead, seeing a world comprised of relationships rather than of people standing alone, a world that coheres through human connection rather than through systems of rules, she finds the puzzle in the dilemma to lie in the failure of the druggist to respond to the wife. Saying that "it is not right for someone to die when their life could be saved," she assumes that if the druggist were to see the consequences of his refusal to lower his price, he would realize that "he should just give it to the wife and then have the husband pay back the money later." Thus she considers the solution to the dilemma to lie in making the wife's condition more salient to the druggist or, that failing, in appealing to others who are in a position to help.

Just as Jake is confident the judge would agree that stealing is the right thing for Heinz to do, so Amy is confident that, "if Heinz and the druggest had talked it out long enough, they could reach something besides stealing." As he considers the law to "have mistakes," so she sees this drama as a mistake, believing that "the world should just share things more and then people wouldn't have to steal." Both children thus recognize the need for agreement but see it as mediated in different ways—he impersonally through systems of logic and law, she personally through communication in relationship. Just as he relies on the conventions of logic to deduce the solution to this dilemma, assuming these conventions to be shared, so she relies on a process of communication, assuming connection and believing that her voice will be heard. Yet while his assumptions about agreement are confirmed by the convergence in logic between his answers and the questions posed, her assumptions are belied by the failure of communication, the interviewer's inability to understand her response.

Although the frustration of the interview with Amy is apparent in the repetition of questions and its ultimate circularity, the problem of interpretation is focused by the assessment of her response. When considered in the light of Kohlberg's definition of the stages and sequence of moral development, her moral judgments appear to be a full stage lower in maturity than those of the boy. Scored as a mixture of stages two and three, her responses seem to reveal a feeling of powerlessness in the world, an inability to think systematically about the concepts of morality or law, a reluctance to challenge authority or to examine the logic of received moral truths, a failure even to conceive of acting directly to save a life or to consider that such action, if taken, could possibly have an effect. As her reliance on relationships seems to reveal a continuing dependence and vulnerability, so her belief in communication as the mode through which to resolve moral dilemmas appears naive and cognitively immature.

Yet Amy's description of herself conveys a markedly different impression. Once again, the hallmarks of the preadolescent child depict a child secure in her sense of herself, confident in the substance of her beliefs, and sure of her ability to do something of value in the world. Describing herself at eleven as "growing and changing," she says that she "sees some things differently now, just because I know myself really well now, and I know a lot more about the world." Yet the world she knows is a different world from that refracted by Kohlberg's construction of Heinz's dilemma. Her world is a world of relationships and psychological truths where an awareness of the connection between people gives rise to a recognition of responsibility for one another, a perception of the need for response. Seen in this light, her understanding of morality as arising from the recognition of relationship, her belief in communication as the mode of conflict resolution, and her conviction that the solution to the dilemma will follow from its compelling representation seem far from naive or cognitively immature. Instead, Amy's judgments contain the insights central to an ethic of care, just as Jake's judgments reflect the logic of the justice approach. Her incipient awareness of the "method of truth," the central tenet of nonviolent conflict resolution, and her belief in the restorative activity of care, lead her to see the actors in the dilemma arrayed not as opponents in a contest of rights but as members of a network of relationships on whose continuation they all depend. Consequently her solution to the dilemma lies in activating the network by communication, securing the inclusion of the wife by strengthening rather than severing connections.

But the different logic of Amy's response calls attention to the interpretation of the interview itself. Conceived as an interrogation, it appears instead as a dialogue, which takes on moral dimensions of its own, pertaining to the interviewer's uses of power and to the manifestations of respect. With this shift in the conception of the interview, it immediately becomes clear that the interviewer's problem in understanding Amy's response stems from the fact that Amy is answering a different question from the one the interviewer thought had been posed. Amy is considering not *whether* Heinz should act in this situation ("*should* Heinz steal the drug?") but rather *how* Heinz should act in response to his awareness of his wife's need ("Should Heinz *steal* the drug?"). The interviewer takes the mode of action for granted, presuming it to be a matter of fact; Amy assumes the necessity for action and considers what form it should take. In the interviewer's failure to imagine a response not dreamt of in Kohlberg's moral philosophy lies the failure to hear Amy's question and to see the logic in her response, to discern that what appears, from one perspective, to be an evasion of the dilemma signifies in other terms a recognition of the problem and a search for a more adequate solution.

Thus in Heinz's dilemma these two children see two very different moral problems—Jake a conflict between life and property that can be resolved by logical deduction, Amy a fracture of human relationship that must be mended with its own thread. Asking different questions that arise from different conceptions of the moral domain, the children arrive at answers that fundamentally diverge, and the arrangement of these answers as successive stages on a scale of increasing moral maturity calibrated by the logic of the boy's response misses the different truth revealed in the judgment of the girl. To the question, "What does he see that she does not?" Kohlberg's theory provides a ready response, manifest in the scoring of Jake's judgments a full stage higher than Amy's in moral maturity; to the question, "What does she see that he does not?" Kohlberg's theory has nothing to say. Since most of her responses fall through the sieve of Kohlberg's scoring system, her responses appear from his perspective to lie outside the moral domain.

Yet just as Jake reveals a sophisticated understanding of the logic of justification, so Amy is equally sophisticated in her understanding of the nature of choice. Recognizing that "if both the roads went in totally separate ways, if you pick one, you'll never know what would happen if you went the other way," she explains that "that's the chance you have to take, and like I said, it's just really a guess." To illustrate her point "in a simple way," she describes her choice to spend the summer at camp:

> I will never know what would have happened if I had stayed here, and if something goes wrong at camp, I'll never know if I stayed here if it would have been better. There's really no way around it because there's no way you can do both at once, so you've got to decide, but you'll never know.

In this way, these two eleven-year-old children, both highly inelligent and perceptive about life, though in different ways, display different modes of moral understanding, different ways of thinking about conflict and choice. In resolving Heinz's dilemma, Jake relies on theft to avoid confrontation and turns to the law to mediate the dispute. Transposing a hierarchy of power into a hierarchy of values, he defuses a potentially explosive conflict between people by casting it as an impersonal conflict of claims. In this way, he abstracts the moral problem from the interpersonal situation, finding in the logic of fairness an objective way to decide who will win the dispute. But this hierarchical ordering, with its imagery of winning and losing and the potential for violence which it contains, gives way in Amy's construction of the dilemma to a network of connection, a web of relationships that is sustained by a process of communication. With this shift, the moral problem changes from one of unfair domination, the imposition of property over life, to one of unnecessary exclusion, the failure of the druggist to respond to the wife.

This shift in the formulation of the moral problem and the concomitant change in the imagery of relationships appear in the responses of two eight-year-old children, Jeffrey and Karen, asked to describe a situation in which they were not sure what was the right thing to do:

Jeffrey	*Karen*
When I really want to go to my friends and my mother is cleaning the cellar, I think about my	I have a lot of friends, and I can't always play with all of them, so everybody's going to

Jeffrey (cont.)	*Karen (cont.)*
friends, and then I think about my mother, and then I think about the right thing to do. (*But how do you know it's the right thing to do?*) Because some things go before other things.	have to take a turn, because they're all my friends. But like if someone's all alone, I'll play with them. (*What kinds of things do you think about when you are trying to make that decision?*) Um, someone all alone, loneliness.

While Jeffrey sets up a hierarchical ordering to resolve a conflict between desire and duty, Karen describes a network of relationships that includes all of her friends. Both children deal with the issues of exclusion and priority created by choice, but while Jeffrey thinks about what goes first, Karen focuses on who is left out.

The contrasting images of hierarchy and network in children's thinking about moral conflict and choice illuminate two views of morality which are complementary rather than sequential or opposed. But this construction of differences goes against the bias of developmental theory toward ordering differences in a hierarchical mode. The correspondence between the order of developmental theory and the structure of the boys' thought contrasts with the disparity between existing theory and the structure manifest in the thought of the girls. Yet in neither comparison does one child's judgment appear as a precursor of the other's position. Thus, questions arise concerning the relation between these perspectives: what is the significance of this difference, and how do these two modes of thinking connect? These questions are elucidated by considering the relationship between the eleven-year-old children's understanding of morality and their descriptions of themselves:

Jake	*Amy*
(*How would you describe yourself to yourself?*)	
Perfect. That's my conceited side. What do you want—any way that I choose to describe myself?	You mean my character? (*What do you think?*) Well, I don't know. I'd describe myself as, well, what do you mean?
(*If you had to describe the person you are in a way that you yourself would know it was you, what would you say?*)	
I'd start off with eleven years old. Jake [last name]. I'd have	Well, I'd say that I was someone who likes school and study-

Jake (cont.)

to add that I live in [town], because that is a big part of me,
and also that my father is a
doctor, because I think that
does change me a little bit, and
that I don't believe in crime,
except for when your name is
Heinz; that I think school is
boring, because I think that
kind of changes your character
a little bit. I don't sort of know
how to describe myself, because
I don't know how to read my
personality. (*If you had to describe the way you actually
would describe yourself, what
would you say?*) I like corny
jokes. I don't really like to get
down to work, but I can do all
the stuff in school. Every single
problem that I have seen in
school I have been able to do,
except for ones that take
knowledge, and after I do the
reading, I have been able to do
them, but sometimes I don't
want to waste my time on easy
homework. And also I'm crazy
about sports. I think, unlike a
lot of people, that the world
still has hope . . . Most people
that I know I like, and I have
the good life, pretty much as
good as any I have seen, and I
am tall for my age.

Amy (cont.)

ing, and that's what I want to
do with my life. I want to be
some kind of a scientist or
something, and I want to do
things, and I want to help people. And I think that's what
kind of person I am, or what
kind of person I try to be. And
that's probably how I'd describe myself. And I want to do
something to help other people.
(*Why is that?*) Well, because I
think that this world has a lot
of problems, and I think that
everybody should try to help
somebody else in some way,
and the way I'm choosing is
through science.

In the voice of the eleven-year-old boy, a familiar form of
self-definition appears, resonating to the inscription of the young
Stephen Daedalus in his geography book: "himself, his name and
where he was," and echoing the descriptions that appear in *Our*

Town, laying out across the coordinates of time and space a hierarchical order in which to define one's place. Describing himself as distinct by locating his particular position in the world, Jake sets himself apart from that world by his abilities, his beliefs, and his height. Although Amy also enumerates her likes, her wants, and her beliefs, she locates herself in relation to the world, describing herself through actions that bring her into connection with others, elaborating ties through her ability to provide help. To Jake's ideal of perfection, against which he measures the worth of himself, Amy counterposes an ideal of care, against which she measures the worth of her activity. While she places herself in relation to the world and chooses to help others through science, he places the world in relation to himself as it defines his character, his position, and the quality of his life.

The contrast between a self defined through separation and a self delineated through connection, between a self measured against an abstract ideal of perfection and a self assessed through particular activities of care, becomes clearer and the implications of this contrast extend by considering the different ways these children resolve a conflict between responsibility to others and responsibility to self. The question about responsibility followed a dilemma posed by a woman's conflict between her commitments to work and to family relationships. While the details of this conflict color the text of Amy's response, Jake abstracts the problem of responsibility from the context in which it appears, replacing the themes of intimate relationship with his own imagery of explosive connection:

Jake	Amy

(When responsibility to oneself and responsibility to others conflict,
how should one choose?)

Jake	Amy
You go about one-fourth to the others and three-fourths to yourself.	Well, it really depends on the situation. If you have a responsibility with somebody else, then you should keep it to a certain extent, but to the extent that it is really going to hurt you or stop you from doing something that you really, really want, then I think maybe you should put yourself first. But if it is your responsibility to

Jake (cont.)

Amy (cont.)
somebody really close to you, you've just got to decide in that situation which is more important, yourself or that person, and like I said, it really depends on what kind of person you are and how you feel about the other person or persons involved.

(Why?)

Because the most important thing in your decision should be yourself, don't let yourself be guided totally by other people, but you have to take them into consideration. So, if what you want to do is blow yourself up with an atom bomb, you should maybe blow yourself up with a hand grenade because you are thinking about your neighbors who would die also.

Well, like some people put themselves and things for themselves before they put other people, and some people really care about other people. Like, I don't think your job is as important as somebody that you really love, like your husband or your parents or a very close friend. Somebody that you really care for—or if it's just your responsibility to your job or somebody that you barely know, then maybe you go first—but if it's somebody that you really love and love as much or even more than you love yourself, you've got to decide what you really love more, that person, or that thing, or yourself. *(And how do you do that?)* Well, you've got to think about it, and you've got to think about both sides, and you've got to think which would be better for everybody or better for yourself, which is more important, and which will make everybody happier. Like if the other people can get

Jake (cont.)	*Amy (cont.)*

<table>
<tr><td></td><td>somebody else to do it, whatever it is, or don't really need you specifically, maybe it's better to do what you want, because the other people will be just fine with somebody else so they'll still be happy, and then you'll be happy too because you'll do what you want.</td></tr>
</table>

(What does responsibility mean?)

It means pretty much thinking of others when I do something, and like if I want to throw a rock, not throwing it at a window, because I thought of the people who would have to pay for that window, not doing it just for yourself, because you have to live with other people and live with your community, and if you do something that hurts them all, a lot of people will end up suffering, and that is sort of the wrong thing to do.	That other people are counting on you to do something, and you can't just decide, "Well, I'd rather do this or that." (*Are there other kinds of responsibility?*) Well, to yourself. If something looks really fun but you might hurt yourself doing it because you don't really know how to do it and your friends say, "Well, come on, you can do it, don't worry," if you're really scared to do it, it's your responsibility to yourself that if you think you might hurt yourself, you shouldn't do it, because you have to take care of yourself and that's your responsibility to yourself.

Again Jake constructs the dilemma as a mathematical equation, deriving a formula that guides the solution: one-fourth to others, three-fourths to yourself. Beginning with his responsibility to himself, a responsibility that he takes for granted, he then considers the extent to which he is responsible to others as well. Proceeding from a premise of separation but recognizing that "you have to live with other people," he seeks rules to limit interference and thus to minimize hurt. Responsibility in his construction pertains to a limitation of action, a restraint of aggression, guided by the recognition that his actions can have effects on others, just as theirs can interfere with him. Thus rules, by limiting interference,

make life in community safe, protecting autonomy through reciprocity, extending the same consideration to others and self.

To the question about conflicting responsibilities, Amy again
responds contextually rather than categorically, saying "it depends"
and indicating how choice would be affected by variations in character and circumstance. Proceeding from a premise of connection,
that "if you have a responsibility *with* somebody else, you should
keep it," she then considers the extent to which she has a responsibility to herself. Exploring the parameters of separation, she imag-
ines situations where, by doing what you want, you would avoid
hurting yourself or where, in doing so, you would not thereby diminish the happiness of others. To her, responsibility signifies response, an extension rather than a limitation of action. Thus it con-
notes an act of care rather than the restraint of aggression. Again
seeking the solution that would be most inclusive of everyone's
needs, she strives to resolve the dilemma in a way that "will make
everybody happier." Since Jake is concerned with limiting interference, while Amy focuses on the need for response, for him the limiting condition is, "Don't let yourself be guided totally by others,"
but for her it arises when "other people are counting on you," in
which case "you can't just decide, 'Well, I'd rather do this or
that.' " The interplay between these responses is clear in that she,
assuming connection, begins to explore the parameters of separation, while he, assuming separation, begins to explore the parameters of connection. But the primacy of separation or connection
leads to different images of self and of relationships.

Most striking among these differences is the imagery of violence in the boy's response, depicting a world of dangerous confrontation and explosive connection, where she sees a world of care
and protection, a life lived with others whom "you may love as
much or even more than you love yourself." Since the conception
of morality reflects the understanding of social relationships, this
difference in the imagery of relationships gives rise to a change in
the moral injunction itself. To Jake, responsibility means *not doing*
what he wants because he is thinking of others; to Amy, it means
doing what others are counting on her to do regardless of what
she herself wants. Both children are concerned with avoiding
hurt but construe the problem in different ways—he seeing hurt
to arise from the expression of aggression, she from a failure
of response.

If the trajectory of development were drawn through either of these children's responses, it would trace a correspondingly different path. For Jake, development would entail coming to see the other as equal to the self and the discovery that equality provides a way of making connection safe. For Amy, development would follow the inclusion of herself in an expanding network of connection and the discovery that separation can be protective and need not entail isolation. In view of these different paths of development and particularly of the different ways in which the experiences of separation and connection are aligned with the voice of the self, the representation of the boy's development as the single line of adolescent growth for both sexes creates a continual problem when it comes to interpreting the development of the girl.

Since development has been premised on separation and told as a narrative of failed relationships—of pre-Oedipal attachments, Oedipal fantasies, preadolescent chumships, and adolescent loves—relationships that stand out against a background of separation, only successively to erupt and give way to an increasingly emphatic individuation, the development of girls appears problematic because of the continuity of relationships in their lives. Freud attributes the turning inward of girls at puberty to an intensification of primary narcissism, signifying a failure of love or "object" relationships. But if this turning inward is construed against a background of continuing connection, it signals a new responsiveness to the self, an expansion of care rather than a failure of relationship. In this way girls, seen not to fit the categories of relationships derived from male experience, call attention to the assumptions about relationships that have informed the account of human development by replacing the imagery of explosive connection with images of dangerous separation.

The significance of this shift is revealed by a study of the images of violence that appear in stories written by college students to pictures on the TAT, a study reporting statistically significant sex differences in the places where violence is seen and in the substance of violent fantasies as well. The themes of separation and connection are central to the study, conducted by Susan Pollak and myself and based on an analysis of stories, written prior to the study, by students as a class exercise in a psychology course on motivation (Pollak and Gilligan, 1982). The study began with Pollak's observation of seemingly bizarre imagery of violence in men's stories about a picture of what appeared to be a tranquil scene, a couple sitting on a bench by a river next to a low bridge. In response to this picture, more than 21 percent of the eighty-eight men in the class had written stories containing incidents of violence—homicide, suicide, stabbing, kidnapping, or rape. In contrast, none of the fifty women in the class had projected violence into this scene.

This observation of violence in men's stories about intimacy appeared to us as a possible corollary to Horner's (1968) report of imagery of violence in women's stories about competitive success. Horner, exemplifying her category of "bizarre or violent imagery" in depicting women's anticipation of negative consequences following success, cites a story that portrays a jubilant Anne, at the top of her medical school class, physically beaten and maimed for life by her jealous classmates. The corollary observation of violent imagery in men's fantasies of intimate relationships is illustrated by a story written by one of the men in the class to the picture of the river-bench scene:

> Nick saw his life pass before his eyes. He could feel the cold penetrating ever deeper into his body. How long had it been since he had fallen through the ice—thirty seconds, a minute? It wouldn't take long for him to succumb to the chilling grip of the mid-February Charles River. What a fool he had been to accept the challenge of his roommate Sam to cross the frozen river. He knew all along that Sam hated him. Hated him for being rich and especially hated him for being engaged to Mary, Sam's childhood sweetheart. But Nick never realized until now that Mary also hated him and really loved Sam. Yet there they were, the two of them, calmly sitting on a bench in the riverbend, watching Nick drown. They'd probably soon be married, and they'd probably finance it with the life insurance policy for which Mary was the beneficiary.

Calling attention to the eye of the observer in noting where danger is seen, Pollak and I wondered whether men and women perceive danger in different situations and construe danger in different ways. Following the initial observation of violence in men's stories about intimacy, we set out to discover whether there were sex differences in the distribution of violent fantasies across situations of achievement and affiliation and whether violence was differentially associated by males and females with intimacy and competitive success. The findings of the resulting images of violence study corroborate previous reports of sex differences in aggression (Terman and Tyler, 1953; Whiting and Pope, 1973; Maccoby and Jacklin, 1974) by revealing a far greater incidence of violence in stories written by men. Of the eighty-eight men in the motivation class, 51 percent wrote at least one story containing images of violence, in comparison to 20 percent of the fifty women in the class, and no woman wrote more than one story in which violence appeared. But the study also revealed sex differences in the distribution and substance of violent fantasies, indicating a difference between the way in which men and women tend to imagine relationships.

Four of the six pictures that comprised the test were chosen for the purposes of this analysis since they provided clear illustrations of achievement and affiliation situations. Two of the pictures show a man and a woman in close personal affiliation—the couple on the bench in the river scene, and two trapeze artists grasping each other's wrists, the man hanging by his knees from the trapeze and the woman in mid-air. Two pictures show people at work in impersonal achievement situations—a man sitting alone at his desk in a high-rise office building, and two women, dressed in white coats, working in a laboratory, the woman in the background watching while the woman in the foreground handles the test tubes. The study centered on a comparison between the stories written about these two sets of pictures.

The men in the class, considered as a group, projected more violence into situations of personal affiliation than they did into impersonal situations of achievement. Twenty-five percent of the men wrote violent stories only to the pictures of affiliation, 19 percent to pictures of both affiliation and achievement, and 7 percent only to pictures of achievement. In contrast, the women saw more violence in impersonal situations of achievement than in situations of affiliation; 16 percent of the women wrote violent stories to the achievement pictures and 6 percent to the pictures of affiliation.

As the story about Nick, written by a man, illustrates the association of danger with intimacy, so the story about Miss Hegstead, written by a woman, exemplifies the projection of violence into situations of achievement and the association of danger with competitive success:

Another boring day in the lab and that mean bitchy Miss Hegstead always breathing down the students' backs. Miss

Hegstead has been at Needham Country High School for 40 years and every chemistry class is the same. She is watching Jane Smith, the model student in the class. She always goes over to Jane and comments to the other students that Jane is always doing the experiment right and Jane is the only student who really works hard, etc. Little does Miss Hegstead know that Jane is making some arsenic to put in her afternoon coffee.

If aggression is conceived as a response to the perception of danger, the findings of the images of violence study suggest that men and women may perceive danger in different social situations and construe danger in different ways—men seeing danger more often in close personal affiliation than in achievement and construing danger to arise from intimacy, women perceiving danger in impersonal achievement situations and construing danger to result from competitive success. The danger men describe in their stories of intimacy is a danger of entrapment or betrayal, being caught in a smothering relationship or humiliated by rejection and deceit. In contrast, the danger women portray in their tales of achievement is a danger of isolation, a fear that in standing out or being set apart by success, they will be left alone. In the story of Miss Hegstead, the only apparent cause of the violence is Jane's being singled out as the best student and thus set apart from her classmates. She retaliates by making arsenic to put in the teacher's afternoon coffee, yet all Miss Hegstead did was to praise Jane for her good work.

As people are brought closer together in the pictures, the images of violence in the men's stories increase, while as people are set further apart, the violence in the women's stories increases. The women in the class projected violence most frequently into the picture of the man at his desk (the only picture portraying a person alone), while the men in the class most often saw violence in the scene of the acrobats on the trapeze (the only picture in which people touched). Thus, it appears that men and women may experience attachment and separation in different ways and that each sex perceives a danger which the other does not see—men in connection, women in separation.

But since the women's perception of danger departs from the usual mode of expectation, the acrobats seeming to be in far greater danger than the man at his desk, their perception calls into question the usual mode of interpretation. Sex differences in aggression are usually interpreted by taking the male response as the norm, so that the absence of aggression in women is identified as the problem to be explained. However, the disparate location of violence in the stories written by women and men raises the question as to why women see the acrobats as safe.

The answer comes from the analysis of the stories about the trapeze. Although the picture of acrobats shows them performing high in the air without a net, 22 percent of the women in the study added nets in the stories they wrote. In contrast, only 6 percent of the men imagined the presence of a net, while 40 percent either explicitly mentioned the absence of a net or implied its absence by describing one or both acrobats as plummeting to their deaths. Thus, the women saw the scene on the trapeze as safe because, by providing nets, they had made it safe, protecting the lives of the acrobats in the event of a fall. Yet failing to imagine the presence of nets in the scene on the trapeze, men, interpreting women's responses, readily attribute the absence of violence in women's stories to a denial of danger or to a repression of aggression (May, 1981) rather than to the activities of care through which the women make the acrobats safe. As women imagine the activities through which relationships are woven and connection sustained, the world of intimacy—which appears so mysterious and dangerous to men—comes instead to appear increasingly coherent and safe.

If aggression is tied, as women perceive, to the fracture of human connection, then the activities of care, as their fantasies suggest, are the activities that make the social world safe, by avoiding isolation and preventing aggression rather than by seeking rules to limit its extent. In this light, aggression appears no longer as an unruly impulse that must be contained but rather as a signal of a fracture of connection, the sign of a failure of relationship. From this perspective, the prevalence of violence in men's fantasies, denoting a world where danger is everywhere seen, signifies a problem in making connection, causing relationships to erupt and turning separation into a dangerous isolation. Reversing the usual mode of interpretation, in which the absence of aggression in women is tied to a problem with separation, makes it possible to see the prevalence of violence in men's stories, its odd location in the context of intimate relationships, and its association with betrayal and deceit as indicative of a problem with connection that leads relationships to become dangerous and safety to appear in separation. Then rule-bound competitive achievement situations, which for women threaten the web of connection, for men provide a mode of connection that establishes clear boundaries and limits aggression, and thus appears comparatively safe.

A story written by one of the women about the acrobats on the trapeze illustrates these themes, calling into question the usual opposition of achievement and affiliation by portraying the continuation of the relationship as the predicate for success:

> These are two Flying Gypsies, and they are auditioning for the big job with the Ringling Brothers Circus. They are the last team to try out for the job, and they are doing very well. They have grace and style, but they use a safety net which some teams do not use. The owners say that they'll hire them if they forfeit the net, but the Gypsies decide that they would rather live longer and turn down the job than take risks like that. They know the act will be ruined if either got hurt and see no sense in taking the risk.

For the Gypsies in the story, it is not the big job with the circus that is of paramount importance but rather the well-being of the two people involved. Anticipating negative consequences from a success attained at the risk of their lives, they forfeit the job rather than the net, protecting their lives but also their act, which "would be ruined if either got hurt."

While women thus try to change the rules in order to preserve relationships, men, in abiding by these rules, depict relationships as easily replaced. Projecting most violence into this scene, they write stories about infidelity and betrayal that end with the male acrobat dropping the woman, presumably replacing the relationship and going on with the act:

> The woman trapeze artist is married to the best friend of the male who has just discovered (before the show) that she has been unfaithful to his friend (her husband). He confronted her with this knowledge and told her to tell her husband but she refused. Not having the courage to confront him himself, the trapeze artist creates an accident while 100 feet above ground, letting the woman slip out of his grasp in mid-flight. She is killed in the incident but he feels no guilt, believing that he has rectified the situation.

The prevalence of violence in male fantasy, like the explosive imagery in the moral judgment of the eleven-year-old boy and the representation of theft as the way to resolve a dispute, is consonant with the view of aggression as endemic in human relationships. But these male fantasies and images also reveal a world where connection is fragmented and communication fails, where betrayal threatens because there seems to be no way of knowing the truth. Asked if he ever thinks about whether or not things are real, eleven-year-old Jake says that he wonders a lot about whether people are telling the truth, about "what people say, like one of my friends says, 'Oh yeah, he said that,' and sometimes I think, 'Is he actually saying the truth?' " Considering truth to lie in math and certainty to reside in logic, he can see "no guidelines" for establishing truth in English class or in personal relationships.

Thus, although aggression has been construed as instinctual and separation has been thought necessary for its constraint, the violence in male fantasy seems rather to arise from a problem in communication and an absence of knowledge about human relationships. But as eleven-year-old Amy sets out to build connection where Kohlberg assumes it will fail, and women in their fantasies create nets of safety where men depict annihilation, the voices of women comment on the problem of aggression that both sexes face, locating the problem in the isolation of self and in the hierarchical construction of human relationships.

Freud, returning in *Civilization and Its Discontents* (1930) to the themes of culture and morality that had preoccupied him as a youth, begins by addressing the standard of measurement, the notion of "what is of true value in life" (p. 64). Referring to a letter from Romain Rolland, who wrote that what is of ultimate comfort to man is a "sensation of 'eternity,' " an "oceanic" feeling, Freud, while honoring his friend, rejects this feeling as an illusion, since he cannot "discover this oceanic feeling in myself." Describing this feeling of "an indissoluble bond, of being one with the external world as a whole," he explains that, "from my own experience I could not convince myself of the primary nature of such a feeling. But this gives me no right to deny that it does not in fact occur in other people. The only question is whether it is being correctly interpreted." Yet raising the question of interpretation, Freud immediately dispels the problem he posed, rejecting the primacy of a feeling of connection on the grounds that "it fits in so badly with the fabric of our psychology." On this basis, he subjects the feeling to a "psychoanalytic—that is, a genetic explanation," deriving the feeling of connection from a more primary feeling of separation (p. 65).

The argument Freud builds centers on the "feeling of our self, of our own ego," which "appears to us as something autonomous and unitary, marked off distinctly from everything else." While he then immediately points out that "such an appearance is deceptive," the deception he sees lies not in the failure to recognize the connection between self and other, but in the failure to see the ego's connection to the unconscious id, "for which it serves as a kind of facade." Turning to the genetic explanation, he traces the feeling of fusion back to the infant's failure to distinguish his ego from the external world as the source of sensation. This distinction arises through the experience of frustration when external sources of sensations evade the infant, "most of all, his mother's breast— and only reappear as a result of his screaming for help" (pp. 65–67). In this screaming for help, Freud sees the birth of the self, the separation of ego from object that leads sensation to be located inside the self while others become objects of gratification.

This disengagement of self from the world outside, however, initiates not only the process of differentiation but also the search for autonomy, the wish to gain control over the sources and objects of pleasure in order to shore up the possibilities for happiness against the risk of disappointment and loss. Thus connection—associated by Freud with "infantile helplessness" and "limitless narcissism," with illusion and the denial of danger—gives way to separation. Consequently, assertion, linked to aggression, becomes the basis for relationships. In this way, a primary separation, arising from disappointment and fueled by rage, creates a self whose relations with others or "objects" must then be protected by rules, a morality that contains this explosive potential and adjusts "the mutual relationships of human beings in the family, the state and the society" (p. 86).

Yet there is an intimation on Freud's part of a sensibility different from his own, of a mental state different from that upon which he premises his psychology, the "single exception" to the "primary mutual hostility of human beings," to the "aggressiveness" that "forms the basis of every relation of affection and love among people," and this exception is located in women's experience, in "the mother's relation to her male child" (p. 113). Once again women appear as the exception to the rule of relationships, by demonstrating a love not admixed with anger, a love arising neither from separation nor from a feeling of being at one with the external world as a whole, but rather from a feeling of connection, a primary bond between other and self. But this love of the mother cannot, Freud says, be shared by the son, who would thus "make himself dependent in a most dangerous way on a portion of the external world, namely his chosen love-object, and expose himself to extreme suffering if he should be rejected by that object or lose it through unfaithfulness or death" (p. 101).

Although Freud, claiming that "we are never so defenceless against suffering as when we love" (p. 82), pursues the line of defense as it leads through anger and conscience to civilization and guilt, the more interesting question would seem to be why the mother is willing to take the risk. Since for her love also creates the possibility of disappointment and loss, the answer would seem to lie in a different experience of connection and a different mode of response. Throughout Freud's work women remain the exception to his portrayal of relationships, and they sound a continuing theme, of an experience of love which, however described—as narcissistic or as hostile to civilization—does not appear to have separation and aggression at its base. In this alternate light, the self appears neither stranded in isolation screaming for help nor lost in fusion with the entire world as a whole, but bound in an indissoluble mode of relationship that is observably different but hard to describe.

Demonstrating a continuing sense of connection in the face of separation and loss, women illuminate an experience of self that, however disparate from Freud's account, speaks directly to the problem of aggression which in the end he confronts, the problem of "how to get rid of the greatest hinderance to civilization," aggressiveness and the defences against it that "cause as much unhappiness as aggression itself" (p. 142–143). In considering this problem, Freud begins to envision its solution in a more primary sense of connection, not an oceanic feeling but an "altruistic urge" that leads to a mode of relationships with others anchored in the "wish for union" with them. While describing the urge toward union with others as antagonistic to individual development (p. 141), Freud intimates a line of development missing from his previous account, a line that leads not through aggression to separation but through differentiation to interdependence. In calling this urge "altruistic," Freud alludes to a different moral conception, arising not to limit aggression but to sustain connection.

Thus alongside the drama Freud creates between happiness and culture in which morality plays the central part, transforming the danger of love into the discomfort of civilization—a drama that darkly illuminates the role of "love in the origin of conscience and the fatal inevitability of the sense of guilt" (p. 132)—another scenario begins to emerge. In this changed light, connection, rather than seeming an illusion or taking on an explosive or transcendental cast, appears as a primary feature of both individual psychology and civilized life. Since "the human individual takes part in the course of the development of mankind at the same time as he pursues his own path in life" (p. 141), separation suddenly begins to appear as illusory as connection formerly had seemed. Yet to incorporate this sense of connection into the fabric of his psychology would change, as Freud sees, not only the coloration of the instinctual life but also the representation of self and the portrayal of relationships.

The "male pattern" of fantasy that Robert May (1980) identifies as "Pride" in his studies of sex differences in projective imagination leads from enhancement to deprivation and continues the story that Freud has told of an initial fracture of connection leading through the experience of separation to an irreparable loss, a glorious achievement followed by a disastrous fall. But the pattern of female fantasy May designates as "Caring" traces a path which remains largely unexplored, a narrative of deprivation followed by enhancement in which connection, though leading through separation, is in the end maintained or restored. Illuminating life as a web rather than a succession of relationships, women portray autonomy rather than attachment as the illusory and dangerous quest. In this way, women's development points toward a different history of human attachment, stressing continuity and change in configuration, rather than replacement and separation, elucidating a different response to loss, and changing the metaphor of growth.

Jean Baker Miller (1976), enumerating the problems that arise when all affiliations are cast in the mould of dominance and subordination, suggests that "the parameters of the female's development are not the same as the male's and that the same terms do not apply" (p. 86). She finds in psychology no language to describe the structuring of women's sense of self, "organized around being able to make and then to maintain affiliations and relationships (p. 83)."

But she sees in this psychic structuring the potential for "more advanced, more affiliative ways of living—less wedded to the dangerous ways of the present," since the sense of self is tied not to a belief in the efficacy of aggression but to a recognition of the need for connection (p. 86). Thus envisioning the potential for a more creative and cooperative mode of life, Miller calls not only for social equality but also for a new language in psychology that would separate the description of care and connection from the vocabulary of inequality and oppression, and she sees this new language as originating in women's experience of relationships.

In the absence of this language, the problem of interpretation that impedes psychologists' understanding of women's experience is mirrored by the problem created for women by the failure to represent their experience or by the distortion in its representation. When the interconnections of the web are dissolved by the hierarchical ordering of relationships, when nets are portrayed as dangerous entrapments, impeding flight rather than protecting against fall, women come to question whether what they have seen exists and whether what they know from their own experience is true. These questions are raised not as abstract philosophical speculations about the nature of reality and truth but as personal doubts that invade women's sense of themselves, compromising their ability to act on their own perceptions and thus their willingness to take responsibility for what they do. This issue becomes central in women's development during the adolescent years, when thought becomes reflective and the problem of interpretation thus enters the stream of development itself.

The two eleven-year-old children, asked to describe their experiences of moral conflict and choice, presage the themes of male and female adolescent development by recounting in one sense the same story but telling it from very different perspectives. Both children describe a situation in school where they confronted a decision of whether or not to tell. For Jake, this dilemma arose when he decided to take action against injustice and seek the enforcement of rules to protect a friend who was being "unfairly" beaten up and hurt. Having gone with his friend to inform the principal of these events, he then wonders whether or not to tell another friend that the principal was told. Since this friend only beat up the other in response to provocation, not telling would subject him to reprisals that would in his case be unjust.

In describing his dilemma, Jake focuses on whether or not it would be right in this instance to violate his standard of trying "to practice what I preach," in this case of keeping his word that no one would know that the principal was told. The quandary hinges on whether or not he can construe his action in telling as fair, whether his various activities of care for the two friends with whom he is involved can be reconciled with the standards of his moral belief. If he can match his action to his standard of justice, then he will not feel "ashamed" and will be "willing to own up" to what he has done; otherwise, he says, he will have to admit to himself and his friends that he has made a mistake.

Amy's dilemma stems from the fact that she saw one friend take a book that belonged to another. Construing the problem as a conflict in loyalties, an issue of responsiveness in relationship, she wonders whether to risk hurting one friend in responding to the hurt of another. Her question is how to act, given what she has seen and knows, since in her construction, not telling as well as telling constitutes a response. As Jake considers violating his standards and going back on his word, compromising his principles out of loyalty to a friend, Amy considers stepping apart from a friendship to assert a standard in which she believes, a standard of sharing and care, of protecting people from hurt. But given this standard, she thinks about the extent to which either friend will be hurt and focuses on the parameters of the situation in order to assess what the likely consequences of her action will be. Just as Jake wonders whether in acting out of friendship he will violate his personal integrity, so Amy worries whether in asserting her beliefs, she will hurt a friend.

In describing her thinking about what to do, Amy recreates the inner dialogue of voices to which she attends—a dialogue that includes the voices of others and also the voice of herself:

> Nobody will ever know I saw, and nobody will hold it against me, but then you start sitting there thinking about it and think that somebody will always know—you'll always know that you never told, and it makes me feel really bad because my friend is sitting there. "Has anybody seen my book? Where is it? Help! I need my book for next class. Help! It's not here. Where is it?" And I think if you know that, it is more important to tell, and you know you're not really tattling or anything, because it's better, you know, to tell.

Just as her awareness of the other's cry for help makes the failure to tell a failure to care, so telling is not tattling when placed in *this* context of relationships. But this contextual mode of analysis leads interpretation readily to shift, since a change in the context of relationships would turn her act of care into an act of betrayal.

In this way, realizing that others may not know what she has seen and heard and recognizing how easily her action can be misconstrued, Amy wonders if it would be better to say nothing or at least not to tell that she told. Thus if the secrets of male adolescence revolve around the harboring of continuing attachments that cannot be represented in the logic of fairness, the secrets of the female adolescent pertain to the silencing of her own voice, a silencing enforced by the wish not to hurt others but also by the fear that, in speaking, her voice will not be heard.

With this silence, the imagery of the Persephone myth returns, charting the mysterious disappearance of the female self in adolescence by mapping an underground world kept secret because it is branded by others as selfish and wrong. When the experience of self and the understanding of morality change with the growth of reflective thought in adolescence, questions about identity and morality converge on the issue of interpretation. As the eleven-year-old girl's question of whether or not to listen to herself extends across the span of adolescence, the difficulty experienced by psychologists in listening to women is compounded by women's difficulty in listening to themselves. This difficulty is evident in a young woman's account of her crisis of identity and moral belief—a crisis that centers on her struggle to disentangle her voice from the voices of others and to find a language that represents her experience of relationships and her sense of herself.

Claire, a participant in the college student study, was interviewed first as a senior in college and then again at the age of twenty-seven. When asked, as a senior, how she would describe herself to herself, she answers "confused," saying that she "should be able to say, 'Well, I'm such and such,'" but instead she finds herself "more unsure now than I think I have ever been." Aware that "people see me in a certain way," she has come to find these images contradictory and constraining, "kind of found myself being pushed, being caught in the middle: I should be a good mother and daughter; I should be, as a college woman, aggressive and high-powered and career-oriented." Yet as the feeling of being caught in the middle has turned, in her senior year, into a sense of being constrained to act, of "being pushed to start making decisions for my-self," she has "come to realize that all these various roles just aren't exactly right." Thus she concludes:

> I am not necessarily the type of girlfriend I should be or that I've been perceived as, and I'm not necessarily the type of daughter that I've been perceived as. You grow up to find yourself in the way other people see you, and it's very hard, all of a sudden, to start separating this and start realizing that really nobody else can make these decisions.

Faced as a senior with the need to make a choice about what to do the following year, she attempts to separate her perception of herself from the perceptions of others, to see herself directly rather than in reflection through others' eyes:

> For a long time, I was seeing myself as other people wanted to see me. I mean, it really appealed to my boyfriend to have a wife who was a professor of English, and I was kind of push-ing it back in my mind that I didn't want to do this; I really felt maybe this is what I really wanted to do. I started seeing all the positive sides of it because I was seeing it through his eyes, and then, suddenly, I kind of realized, I can't do this anymore. And I can't, you know, I've got to stop this and see myself as I want to see *it,* and then I realized that no, this is very stuffy, and this world of academia isn't necessarily *right for me,* even though I would be the ideal wife in that situation. So then I am naturally faced with what is right for me, and it's very hard, because at the same time, I'm faced with a feel-ing that I can't grow up.

Thus, as her way of looking at herself becomes more direct, the moral question correspondingly shifts from what is "right" to what is "right for me." Yet in facing that challenge, she immediately draws back as she encounters the feeling "that I can't grow up."

Caught by the interviewer's request for self-description at a time when she is resisting "categorizing or classifying myself," she finds it "hard to start defining what I'm in the process of undefin-ing," the self that, in the past, would "try to push my feelings under the rug" so as not to create any "repercussions." Describing herself as "loving," she is caught between the two contexts in which that term now applies: an underground world that sets her "apart from others, apart from their definitions of me," and a world of connections that sets her apart from herself. In trying to explain her sense of herself as at once separate and connected, she encounters a problem with "terminology" when trying to convey a new understanding of both self and relationship:

> I'm trying to tell you two things. I'm trying to be myself alone, apart from others, apart from their definitions of me, and yet at the same time I'm doing just the opposite, trying to be with or relate to—whatever the terminology is—I don't think they are mutually exclusive.

In this way she ties a new sense of separation to a new experience of connection, a way of being with others that allows her also to be with herself.

Reaching for an image that would convey this uncharted sense of connection but unable to find one herself, she seizes on one offered by a friend, the character of Gudrun in D. H. Lawrence's *Women in Love.* The image of Gudrun evokes for Claire her sense of being "childish" and "untamed," responsive to the sensuality both in nature and in herself. This connection to the world of "sensual enjoyment" represents the "artistic and bohemian" side of herself and contrasts with the view of herself as "ladylike and well brought-up." Yet the image of Gudrun, despite its evocation of a different form of connection, is in the end morally problematic for her because it implies being "uncaring of others."

Again Claire is caught, but in a different way, not between the contradictory expectations of others but between a responsiveness to others and to herself. Sensing that these modes of response "aren't mutually exclusive," she examines the moral judgment that in the past kept them apart. Formerly, she considered "a moral way of looking" to be one that focused on "responsibility to others"; now she has come to question what seemed in the past a self-evident truth, that "in doing what's right for others, you're doing what's right for yourself." She has, she says, "reached the point where I don't think I can be any good to anyone unless I know who I am."

In the process of seeking to "discover what's me," she has begun to "get rid of all these labels and things I just don't see on my own," to separate her perceptions from her former mode of interpretation and to look more directly at others as well as herself. Thus, she has come to observe "faults" in her mother, whom she perceives as endlessly giving, "because she doesn't care if she hurts herself in doing it. She doesn't realize—well, she does realize, that in hurting herself, she hurts people very close to her." Measured against a standard of care, Claire's ideal of self-sacrifice gives way to a vision of "a family where everyone is encouraged to become an individual and at the same time everybody helps others and receives help from them."

Bringing this perspective to Heinz's dilemma, Claire identifies the same moral problem as the eleven-year-old Amy, focusing not on the conflict of rights but on the failure of response. Claire believes that Heinz should steal the drug ("His wife's life was much more important than anything. He should have done anything to save her life"), but she counters the rights construction with her own interpretation. Although the druggist "had a right, I mean he had the legal right, I also think he had the moral obligation to show compassion in this case. I don't think he had the right to refuse." In tying the necessity for Heinz's action to the fact that "the wife needed him at this point to do it; she couldn't have done it, and it's up to him to do for her what she needs," Claire elaborates the same concept of responsibility that was articulated by Amy. They both equate responsibility with the need for response that arises from the recognition that others are counting on you and that you are in a position to help.

Whether Heinz loves his wife or not is irrelevant to Claire's decision, not because life has priority over affection, but because his wife "is another human being who needs help." Thus the moral injunction to act stems not from Heinz's feelings about his wife but from his awareness of her need, an awareness mediated not by identification but by a process of communication. Just as Claire considers the druggist morally responsible for his refusal, so she ties morality to the awareness of connection, defining the moral person as one who, in acting, "seriously considers the consequences to everybody involved." Therefore, she criticizes her mother for "neglecting her responsibility to herself" at the same time that she criticizes herself for neglecting her responsibility to others.

Although Claire's judgments of Heinz's dilemma for the most part do not fit the categories of Kohlberg's scale, her understanding of the law and her ability to articulate its function in a systematic way earn her a moral maturity score of stage four. Five years later, when she is interviewed at the age of twenty-seven, this score is called into question because she subsumes the law to the considerations of responsibility that informed her thinking about the druggist, Heinz, and his wife. Judging the law now in terms of whom it protects, she extends her ethic of responsibility to a broader vision of societal connection. But the disparity between this vision and the justice conception causes her score on Kohlberg's scale to regress.

During the time when Claire's moral judgments appeared to regress, her moral crisis was resolved. Having taken Kohlberg's course, she suspected that what she had experienced as growth was no progress in his terms. Thus, when she received the letter asking if she would be willing to be interviewed again, she thought:

> My God, what if I have regressed. It seems to me that at one stage of my life, I would have been able to answer these dilemmas with a lot more surety and said, "Yes, this is absolutely right and this is absolutely wrong." And I am just sinking deeper and deeper into the mire of uncertainty. I am not sure if that is good or bad at this point, but I think there has been, in that sense, a direction.

Contrasting an absolute standard of judgment with her own experience of the complexity of moral choice, she introduces the question of direction, the interpretation of her own development.

The question of interpretation recurs throughout the text of her interview at age twenty-seven when, married and about to start medical school, she reflects on her experience of crisis and describes the changes in her life and thought. Speaking of the present, she says that "things have fallen into place," but immediately corrects her phrasing since "that sounds like somebody else put them together, and that's not what happened." The problem of interpretation, however, centers on describing the mode of connection. The connection itself is apparent in Claire's description of herself which she says, "sounds sort of strange," as she characterizes herself as "maternal, with all its connotations." Envisioning herself "as a physician, as a mother," she says that "it's hard for me to think about myself without thinking about other people around me that I am giving to." Like Amy, Claire ties her experience of self to activities of care and connection. Joining the image of her mother with that of herself, she sees herself as a maternal physician, as preparing, like Amy, to become a scientist who takes care of the world.

In describing the resolution of a crisis that extended over a period of years, she retraces her steps in order to explain her discovery of "a direction underlying it all." The crisis began in her sophomore year in college:

> For an entire weekend I didn't get out of bed because there was no reason to. I just couldn't bring myself to get out of bed. I didn't know what I would do if I got out of bed, but most of my sophomore year was like that. I didn't know what I was doing, what the reason for doing anything was. Nothing seemed to connect together.

Tying her despair to her sense of disconnection, she casts about for a word or image to fit the experience:

> It wasn't a turning point in that, when I got out of bed, everything was right again. That didn't happen. It wasn't a great epiphany or anything like that. It just sticks out in my mind, even though at the time it didn't seem like a powerful experience. It did not seem like anything was happening to me. No. It seems like it was a very powerful experience. It was real.

In measuring her own experience against existing metaphors of crisis and change, she begins to conclude that nothing had happened, or that what happened was not powerful or real. She did not hit rock bottom, nor did she experience an epiphany or "ultimate despair":

> I didn't lie in bed and think my life is so totally worthless. It wasn't that. It wasn't like profound unhappiness. It was just nothing. Maybe that is the ultimate despair, but you don't feel it at the time. I guess that sticks out as one thing because it was so devoid of feeling. Another thing was the extreme bitterness and extreme hatred I felt toward [a relative] who abandoned the family. I mean it was just the opposite; it was so intense.

Finding, in both the absence of feeling and in the presence of hatred, no way to connect with others, she interprets her experience of despair as arising from the sense of disconnection that ensued, in part, from the failure of family relationships.

The feeling of disconnection from others leads Claire to struggle to see herself as "worthwhile," as worthy of her own care and thus as justified in acting on her own behalf. As she describes the process through which she came to risk doing what she wanted to do, she indicates how in this process her conception of morality changed. Whereas she used to define the good person as "the person who does the most good for others," now she ties morality to the understanding that arises from the experience of relationship, since she considers the capacity "to understand what someone else is experiencing" as the prerequisite for moral response.

Impatient now with Heinz's dilemma, she structures it starkly as a contrast between the wife's life and the druggist's greed, seeing in the druggist's preoccupation with profit a failure of understanding as well as of response. Life is worth more than money because "everybody has the right to live." But then she shifts her perspective, saying, "I'm not sure I should phrase it that way." In her rephrasing, she replaces the hierarchy of rights with a web of relationships. Through this replacement, she challenges the premise of separation underlying the notion of rights and articulates a "guiding principle of connection." Perceiving relationships as primary rather than as derived from separation, considering the interdependence of people's lives, she envisions "the way things are" and "the way things should be" as a web of interconnection where "everybody belongs to it and you all come from it." Against this conception of social reality, the druggist's claim stands in fundamental contradiction. Seeing life as dependent on connection, as sustained by activities of care, as based on a bond of attachment rather than a contract of agreement, she believes that Heinz should steal the drug, whether or not he loves his wife, "by virtue of the fact that they are both there." Although a person may not like someone else, "you have to love someone else, because you are inseparable from them. In a way it's like loving your right hand; it is part of you. That other person is part of that giant collection of everybody." Thus she articulates an ethic of responsibility that stems from an awareness of interconnection: "The stranger is still another person belonging to that group, people you are connected to by virtue of being another person."

Claire describes morality as "the constant tension between being part of something larger and a sort of self-contained entity," and she sees the ability to live with that tension as the source of moral character and strength. This tension is at the center of the moral dilemmas she has faced which were conflicts of responsibility that pertained to an issue of truth and turned on the recognition of relationship. The problem of truth became apparent to her when, after college, she worked as a counselor in an abortion clinic and was told that, if a woman wanted to see what was evacuated from her uterus, she should be told, "You can't see anything now. It just looks like jelly at this point." Since this description clashed with the moral turmoil Claire felt while working at the clinic, she decided that she "had to face up to what was going on." Thus, she decided to look at a fetus evacuated in a late abortion, and in doing so, she came to the realization that:

> I just couldn't kid myself anymore and say there was nothing in the uterus, just a tiny speck. This is not true, and I knew it wasn't true, but I sort of had to see it. And yet at the same time I knew that's what was going on. I also believed that it was right; it should have happened. But I couldn't say, "Well, this is right and this is wrong." I was just constantly torn.

When she measured the world by eye and relied on her perceptions in defining what was happening and what was true, the absolutes of moral judgment dissolved. As a result, she was "constantly torn" and mired in uncertainty with respect to the issue of abortion, but she was also able to act in a more responsible way:

> I struggled with it a whole lot. Finally, I just had to reconcile myself—I really do believe this, but it is not an easy thing that you can say without emotions and maybe regret—that, yes, life is sacred, but the quality of life is also important, and it has to be the determining thing in this particular case. The quality of that mother's life, the quality of an unborn child's life—I have seen too many pictures of babies in trash cans and that sort of thing, and it is so easy to say, "Well, either/or," and it just isn't like that. And I had to be able to say, "Yes, this is killing, there is no way around it, but I am willing to accept that, but I am willing to go ahead with it, and it's hard." I don't think I can explain it. I don't think I can really verbalize the justification.

Claire's inability to articulate her moral position stems in part from the fact that hers is a contextual judgment, bound to the particulars of time and place, contingent always on "that mother" and that "unborn child" and thus resisting a categorical formulation. To her, the possibilities of imagination outstrip the capacity for generalization. But this sense of being unable to verbalize or explain the rationale for her participation in abortion counseling, an inability that could reflect the inadequacy of her moral thought, could also reflect the fact that she finds in the world no validation of the position she is trying to convey, a position that is neither pro-life nor pro-choice but based on a recognition of the continuing connection between the life of the mother and the life of the child.

Thus Claire casts the dilemma not as a contest of rights but as a problem of relationships, centering on a question of responsibility which in the end must be faced. If attachment cannot be sustained, abortion may be the better solution, but in either case morality lies in recognizing connection, taking responsibility for the abortion decision or taking responsibility for the care of the child. Although there are times when "killing like that is necessary, it shouldn't become too easy," as it does "if it is removed from you. If the fetus is just jelly, that is removed from you. Southeast Asia is further removed from you." Thus morality and the preservation of life are contingent on sustaining connection, seeing the consequences of action by keeping the web of relationships intact, "not allowing somebody else to do the killing for you without taking the responsibility." Again an absolute judgment yields to the complexity of relationships. The fact that life is sustained by connection leads her to affirm the "sacred tie" of life rather than "the sacredness of life at all costs," and to articulate an ethic of responsibility while remaining cognizant of the issue of rights.

The problem of truth also arose for Claire when a friend asked her to write a peer recommendation for a job, creating a dilemma similar to the one that Amy described. While Amy wondered whether "to keep friendship or keep justice," though in the end the question became one of responding to others and thus keeping peace with herself, the matter of honesty was from the beginning at the center of Claire's concern: "How could I be honest and at the same time do her justice?" But the issue of justice was an issue of responsibility, arising from the recognition that her actions in forming the friendship had set up a chain of expectations, leading her friend to believe that she could count on Claire for help. Claire, realizing that she "really didn't like" her friend and that their value systems were "very different," also recognized the reality of the relationship and the impossibility of being both honest and fair. The question of what to do hinged on a judgment of the relative hurt her actions would cause, to the friend and to the people whose lives would be affected if the friend succeeded in getting the job. Deciding that in this situation, writing the letter was the better solution, she realized the dilemma could have been avoided by "being a little more honest with her from day one."

With the question of honesty, Claire comes in the end to the drama of "Mr. Right" and "Mr. Wrong," a drama that joins the various themes of relationship, responsibility, and interpretation by personalizing the question of moral truth rather than objectifying the issue of personal relationships. Mr. Right, like Anne in Horner's story, was at the top of his medical school class and "hated not to have all his Sunday to study," given his wish to stay at the top. Consequently, on Saturday nights he would return to sleep on his own bed, leaving Claire feeling not only alone and abandoned but also "selfish" and "wrong":

> What is wrong with me that I want more? There is obviously something. I am a terribly selfish person, and I never really faced the fact that there was something obviously wrong with the relationship.

As a result of this experience, she began to suspect that Mr. Right was not "right for me." But unwilling to end the relationship, she turned instead to Mr. Wrong:

> By senior year, it just blew, but instead of saying, "I am asserting myself, I am not going to stand for this any longer," I had this very sordid affair behind his back and then threw it up to him. And not only threw it up to him, but went to him in tears and confessed, which felt wonderful, but it was all sort of subconsciously calculated to hurt him.

Claire first describes the conflict or the dilemma as a disparity between judgment and action, given her "very strict kind of in a funny way monogamous feelings," but then adds that the real conflict was between two images of herself, "this virginal pure thing and this other side of myself that was sort of starting to blossom." The problem arose because she "was not able to make a decision at that point of what I wanted to do." Stranded between two images of herself, she was caught between two worlds of relationship:

> I was not willing to give up the first relationship because it represented a lot of things. This was Mr. Right to everybody else but me who knew better. And the other guy, who clearly was, in contrast, Mr. Wrong, sort of represented that same sort of animal thing to me at that time, and I wasn't able to give that up either.

As she began to confront the disparity within her perception of herself, she also began "to see that moral standards imposed by somebody else aren't necessarily right for me." Thus, as Mr. Right turned out not to be right, so Mr. Wrong was not so wrong.

Focusing on her actions that revealed the unresolved conflict within herself, she says that "the two people involved in that conflict were myself and myself." As she explores the inner division, she explores the world of relationships as well, identifying her unwillingness to "take responsibility for my actions" as having perpetuated a cycle of hurt:

> That was part of the whole problem with the relationship, my not taking responsibility for my part of it. It was also, I think, sort of designed to hurt him as deeply as he hurt me, even though I had never taken the responsibility for having him stop hurting me. I never said, "You stay here this Saturday or else this is the end of the relationship." Only two or three years later did I realize what was going on.

Claire, looking back on the dilemma of Mr. Right and Mr. Wrong, locates the problem not only in her failure to assert herself but also in "not understanding that I *should* be asserting myself." But the act of assertion is an act not of aggression but rather of communication. By telling Mr. Right the truth about herself, she would not only have prevented aggression but also have provided an opportunity for response. As the "I" who spoke clearly at eleven becomes in adolescence "confused," so the resolution of that confusion occurs through the discovery that responsiveness to self and responsiveness to others are connected rather than opposed.

Describing the people whom she admires—her mother for

being "as giving as she is," her husband who "lives by what he believes"—Claire envisions for herself a life of integrity centered on activities of care. This vision is illuminated by the actions of a woman physician who, seeing the loneliness of an old woman in the hospital, "would go out and buy her a root beer float and sit at her bedside just so there would be somebody there for her." The ideal of care is thus an activity of relationship, of seeing and responding to need, taking care of the world by sustaining the web of connection so that no one is left alone.

While the truths of psychological theory have blinded psychologists to the truth of women's experience, that experience illuminates a world which psychologists have found hard to trace, a territory where violence is rare and relationships appear safe. The reason women's experience has been so difficult to decipher or even discern is that a shift in the imagery of relationships gives rise to a problem of interpretation. The images of hierarchy and web, drawn from the texts of men's and women's fantasies and thoughts, convey different ways of structuring relationships and are associated with different views of morality and self. But these images create a problem in understanding because each distorts the other's representation. As the top of the hierarchy becomes the edge of the web and as the center of a network of connection becomes the middle of a hierarchical progression, each image marks as dangerous the place which the other defines as safe. Thus the images of hierarchy and web inform different modes of assertion and response: the wish to be alone at the top and the consequent fear that others will get too close; the wish to be at the center of connection and the consequent fear of being too far out on the edge. These disparate fears of being stranded and being caught give rise to different portrayals of achievement and affiliation, leading to different modes of action and different ways of assessing the consequences of choice.

The reinterpretation of women's experience in terms of their own imagery of relationships thus clarifies that experience and also provides a nonhierarchical vision of human connection. Since relationships, when cast in the image of hierarchy, appear inherently unstable and morally problematic, their transposition into the image of web changes an order of inequality into a structure of interconnection. But the power of the images of hierarchy and web, their evocation of feelings and their recurrence in thought, signifies the embeddedness of both of these images in the cycle of human life. The experiences of inequality and interconnection, inherent in the relation of parent and child, then give rise to the ethics of justice and care, the ideals of human relationship—the vision that self and other will be treated as of equal worth, that despite differences in power, things will be fair; the vision that everyone will be responded to and included, that no one will be left alone or hurt. These disparate visions in their tension reflect the paradoxical truths of human experience—that we know ourselves as separate only insofar as we live in connection with others, and that we experience relationship only insofar as we differentiate other from self.

3 Concepts of Self and Morality

A COLLEGE STUDENT, responding to the question "If you had to say what morality meant to you, how would you sum it up?" replies:

When I think of the word *morality,* I think of obligations. I usually think of it as conflicts between personal desires and social things, social considerations, or personal desires of yourself versus personal desires of another person or people or whatever. Morality is that whole realm of how you decide these conflicts. A moral person is one who would decide by placing themselves more often than not as equals. A truly moral person would always consider another person as their equal . . . In a situation of social interaction, something is morally wrong where the individual ends up screwing a lot of people. And it is morally right when everyone comes out better off.

Yet when asked if she can think of someone whom she considers a genuinely moral person, she replies, "Well, immediately I think of Albert Schweitzer, because he has obviously given his life to help others." Obligation and sacrifice override the ideal of equality, setting up a basic contradiction in her thought.

Another undergraduate responds to the question "What does it mean to say something is morally right or wrong?" by also speaking first of responsibilities and obligations:

It has to do with responsibilities and obligations and values, mainly values ... In my life situation I relate morality with interpersonal relationships that have to do with respect for the other person and myself. (*Why respect other people?*) Because they have a consciousness or feelings that can be hurt, an awareness that can be hurt.

The concern about hurting others persists as a major theme in the responses of two other women students to the question "Why be moral?"

Millions of people have to live together peacefully. I personally don't want to hurt other people. That's a real criterion, a main criterion for me. It underlies my sense of justice. It isn't nice to inflict pain. I empathize with anyone in pain. Not hurting others is important in my own private morals. Years ago I would have jumped out of a window not to hurt my boyfriend. That was pathological. Even today, though, I want approval and love, and I don't want enemies. Maybe that's why there is morality—so people can win approval, love, and friendship.

My main principle is not hurting other people as long as you aren't going against your own conscience and as long as you remain true to yourself ... There are many moral issues, such as abortion, the draft, killing, stealing, monogamy. If something is a controversial issue like these, then I always say it is up to the individual. The individual has to decide and then follow his own conscience. There are no moral absolutes. Laws are pragmatic instruments, but they are not absolutes. A viable society can't make exceptions all the time, but I would personally ... I'm afraid I'm heading for some big crisis with my boyfriend someday, and someone will get hurt, and he'll get more hurt than I will. I feel an obligation not to hurt him, but also an obligation not to lie. I don't know if it is possible not to lie and not to hurt.

The common thread that runs through these statements is the wish not to hurt others and the hope that in morality lies a way of solving conflicts so that no one will be hurt. This theme is independently introduced by each of the four women as the most specific item in their response to a most general question. The moral person is one who helps others; goodness is service, meeting one's obligations and responsibilities to others, if possible without sacrificing oneself. While the first of the four women ends by denying the conflict she initially introduced, the last woman anticipates a conflict between remaining true to herself and adhering to her principle of not hurting others. The dilemma that would test the limits of this judgment would be one where helping others is seen to be at the price of hurting the self.

The reticence about taking stands on "controversial issues," a willingness to "make exceptions all the time," is echoed repeatedly by other college women:

> I never feel that I can condemn anyone else. I have a very relativistic position. The basic idea that I cling to is the sanctity of human life. I am inhibited about impressing my beliefs on others.

> I could never argue that my belief on a moral question is anything that another person should accept. I don't believe in absolutes. If there is an absolute for moral decisions, it is human life.

Or as a thirty-one-year-old graduate student says when explaining why she would find it difficult to steal a drug to save her own life, despite her belief that it would be right to steal for another: "It's just very hard to defend yourself against the rules. I mean, we live by consensus, and if you take an action simply for yourself, by yourself, there's no consensus there, and that is relatively indefensible in this society now."

What emerges in these voices is a sense of vulnerability that impedes these women from taking a stand, what George Eliot regards as the girl's "susceptibility" to adverse judgments by others, which stems from her lack of power and consequent inability "to do something in the world" (p. 365). The unwillingness to make moral judgments that Kohlberg and Kramer (1969) and Kohlberg and Gilligan (1971) associate with the adolescent crisis of identity and belief takes the form in men of calling into question the concept of morality itself. But these women's reluctance to judge stems rather from their uncertainty about their right to make moral statements, or perhaps from the price for them that such judgment seems to entail.

When women feel excluded from direct participation in society, they see themselves as subject to a consensus or judgment made and enforced by the men on whose protection and support they depend and by whose names they are known. A divorced middle-aged woman, mother of adolescent daughters, resident of a sophisticated university community, tells the story:

> As a woman, I feel I never understood that I was a person, that I could make decisions and I had a right to make decisions. I always felt that that belonged to my father or my husband in some way, or church, which was always represented by a male clergyman. They were the three men in my life: father, husband, and clergyman, and they had much more to say about what I should or shouldn't do. They were really authority figures which I accepted. It only lately has occurred to me that I never even rebelled against it, and my girls are much more conscious of this, not in the militant sense, but just in the recognizing sense ... I still let things happen to me rather than make them happen, than make choices, although I know all about choices. I know the procedures and the steps and all. (*Do you have any clues about why this might be true?*) Well, I think in one sense there is less responsibility involved. Because if you make a dumb decision, you have to take the rap. If it happens to you, well, you can complain about it. I think that if you don't grow up feeling that you ever have any choices, you don't have the sense that you have emotional responsibility. With this sense of choice comes this sense of responsibility.

The essence of moral decision is the exercise of choice and the willingness to accept responsibility for that choice. To the extent that women perceive themselves as having no choice, they correspondingly excuse themselves from the responsibility that decision entails. Childlike in the vulnerability of their dependence and consequent fear of abandonment, they claim to wish only to please, but in return for their goodness they expect to be loved and cared for. This, then, is an "altruism" always at risk, for it presupposes an innocence constantly in danger of being compromised by an awareness of the trade-off that has been made. Asked to describe herself, a college senior responds:

> I have heard of the onion-skin theory. I see myself as an onion, as a block of different layers. The external layers are

for people that I don't know that well, the agreeable, the social, and as you go inward, there are more sides for people I
know that I show. I am not sure about the innermost, whether
there is a core, or whether I have just picked up everything as
I was growing up, these different influences. I think I have a
neutral attitude toward myself, but I do think in terms of good
and bad. Good—I try to be considerate and thoughtful of
other people, and I try to be fair in situations and be tolerant.
I use the words, but I try and work them out practically. Bad
things—I am not sure if they are bad, if they are altruistic or I
am doing them basically for approval of other people. (*Which
things are these?*) The values that I try to act out. They deal
mostly with interpersonal relations . . . If I were doing things
for approval, it would be a very tenuous thing. If I didn't get
the right feedback, there might go all my values.

Ibsen's play *A Doll's House* depicts the explosion of just such
a world through the eruption of a moral dilemma that calls into
question the notion of goodness which lies at its center. Nora, the
"squirrel wife," living with her husband as she lived with her father, puts into action this conception of goodness as sacrifice and,
with the best of intentions, takes the law into her own hands. The
crisis that ensues, most painfully for her in the repudiation of that
goodness by the very person who was its recipient and beneficiary,
causes her to reject the suicide that she initially saw as its ultimate
expression and to choose instead to seek new and firmer answers to
questions of identity and moral belief.

The availability of choice, and with it the onus of responsibility, has now invaded the most private sector of the woman's domain and threatens a similar explosion. For centuries, women's sexuality anchored them in passivity, in a receptive rather than an
active stance, where the events of conception and childbirth could
be controlled only by a withholding in which their own sexual
needs were either denied or sacrificed. That such a sacrifice entailed
a cost to their intelligence as well was seen by Freud (1908) when
he tied the "undoubted intellectual inferiority of so many women"
to "the inhibition of thought necessitated by sexual suppression" (p.
199). The strategies of withholding and denial that women have
employed in the politics of sexual relations appear similar to their
evasion or withholding of judgment in the moral realm. The hesi-
tance of college students to assert a belief even in the value of

human life, like the reluctance to claim one's sexuality, bespeaks a self uncertain of its strength, unwilling to deal with choice, and avoiding confrontation.

Thus women have traditionally deferred to the judgment of men, although often while intimating a sensibility of their own which is at variance with that judgment. Maggie Tulliver in *The Mill on the Floss* responds to the accusations that ensue from the discovery of her secretly continued relationship with Phillip Wakeham by acceding to her brother's moral judgment, while at the same time asserting a different set of standards by which she attests to her own superiority:

> I don't want to defend myself . . . I know I've been wrong—often continually. But yet, sometimes when I have done wrong, it has been because I have feelings that you would be the better for if you had them. If *you* were in fault ever, if you had done anything very wrong, I should be sorry for the pain it brought you; I should not want punishment to be heaped on you.

Maggie's protest is an eloquent assertion of the age-old split between thinking and feeling, justice and mercy, that underlies many of the clichés and stereotypes concerning the difference between the sexes. But considered from another point of view, her protest signifies a moment of confrontation, replacing a former evasion. This confrontation reveals two modes of judging, two different constructions of the moral domain—one traditionally associated with masculinity and the public world of social power, the other with femininity and the privacy of domestic interchange. The developmental ordering of these two points of view has been to consider the masculine as more adequate than the feminine and thus as replacing the feminine when the individual moves toward maturity. The reconciliation of these two modes, however, is not clear.

Norma Haan's (1975) research on college students and Constance Holstein's (1976) three-year study of adolescents and their parents indicate that the moral judgments of women differ from those of men in the greater extent to which women's judgments are tied to feelings of empathy and compassion and are concerned with the resolution of real as opposed to hypothetical dilemmas. However, as long as the categories by which development is assessed are derived from research on men, divergence from the masculine standard can be seen only as a failure of development. As a result, the thinking of women is often classified with that of children. The absence of alternative criteria that might better encompass the development of women, however, points not only to the limitations of theories framed by men and validated by research samples disproportionately male and adolescent, but also to the diffidence prevalent among women, their reluctance to speak publicly in their own voice, given the constraints imposed on them by their lack of power and the politics of relations between the sexes.

In order to go beyond the question, "How much like men do women think, how capable are they of engaging in the abstract and hypothetical construction of reality?" it is necessary to identify and define developmental criteria that encompass the categories of women's thought. Haan points out the necessity to derive such criteria from the resolution of the "more frequently occurring, real-life moral dilemmas of interpersonal, empathic, fellow-feeling concerns" (p. 34) which have long been the center of women's moral concern. But to derive developmental criteria from the language of women's moral discourse, it is necessary first to see whether women's construction of the moral domain relies on a language different from that of men and one that deserves equal credence in the definition of development. This in turn requires finding places where women have the power to choose and thus are willing to speak in their own voice.

When birth control and abortion provide women with effective means for controlling their fertility, the dilemma of choice enters a central arena of women's lives. Then the relationships that have traditionally defined women's identities and framed their moral judgments no longer flow inevitably from their reproductive capacity but become matters of decision over which they have control. Released from the passivity and reticence of a sexuality that binds them in dependence, women can question with Freud what it is that they want and can assert their own answers to that question. However, while society may affirm publicly the woman's right to choose for herself, the exercise of such choice brings her privately into conflict with the conventions of femininity, particularly the moral equation of goodness with self-sacrifice. Although independent assertion in judgment and action is considered to be the hallmark of adulthood, it is rather in their care and concern for others that women have both judged themselves and been judged.

The conflict between self and other thus constitutes the central moral problem for women, posing a dilemma whose resolution requires a reconciliation between femininity and adulthood. In the absence of such a reconciliation, the moral problem cannot be resolved. The "good woman" masks assertion in evasion, denying responsibility by claiming only to meet the needs of others, while the "bad woman" forgoes or renounces the commitments that bind her in self-deception and betrayal. It is precisely this dilemma—the conflict between compassion and autonomy, between virtue and power—which the feminine voice struggles to resolve in its effort to reclaim the self and to solve the moral problem in such a way that no one is hurt.

When a woman considers whether to continue or abort a pregnancy, she contemplates a decision that affects both self and others and engages directly the critical moral issue of hurting. Since the choice is ultimately hers and therefore one for which she is responsible, it raises precisely those questions of judgment that have been most problematic for women. Now she is asked whether she wishes to interrupt that stream of life which for centuries has immersed her in the passivity of dependence while at the same time imposing on her the responsibility for care. Thus the abortion decision brings to the core of feminine apprehension, to what Joan Didion (1972) calls "the irreconcilable difference of it—that sense of living one's deepest life underwater, that dark involvement with blood and birth and death" (p. 14), the adult questions of responsibility and choice.

How women deal with such choices was the subject of the abortion study, designed to clarify the ways in which women construct and resolve abortion decisions. Twenty-nine women, ranging in age from fifteen to thirty-three and diverse in ethnic background and social class, were referred for the study by abortion and pregnancy counseling services. The women participated in the study for a variety of reasons—some to gain further clarification with respect to a decision about which they were in conflict, some in response to a counselor's concern about repeated abortions, and others to contribute to ongoing research. Although the pregnancies occurred under a variety of circumstances in the lives of these women, certain commonalities were discerned. The adolescents often failed to use birth control because they denied or discredited their capacity to bear children. Some women became pregnant due to the omission of contraceptive measures in circumstances where intercourse had not been anticipated. Some pregnancies coincided with efforts on the part of the women to end a relationship and may be seen as a manifestation of ambivalence or as a way of putting the relationship to the ultimate test of commitment. For these women, the pregnancy appeared to be a way of testing truth, making the baby an ally in the search for male support and protection or, that failing, a companion victim of male rejection. Finally, some women became pregnant as a result either of a failure of birth control or of a joint decision that was later reconsidered. Of the twenty-nine women, four decided to have the baby, two miscarried, twenty-one chose abortion, and two who were in doubt about the decision at the time of the interview could not be contacted for the follow-up research.

The women were interviewed twice, first at the time they were making the decision, in the first trimester of a confirmed pregnancy, and then at the end of the following year. The referral procedure required that there be an interval between the woman's contacting a counselor or clinic and the time the abortion was performed. Given this factor and the fact that some counselors saw participation in the study as an effective means of crisis-intervention, there is reason to believe that the women interviewed were in greater than usual conflict over the decision. Since the study focused on the relation between judgment and action rather than on the issue of abortion per se, no effort was made to select a sample that would be representative of women considering, seeking, or having abortions. Thus the findings pertain to the different ways in which women think about dilemmas in their lives rather than to the ways in which women in general think about the abortion choice.

In the initial part of the interview, the women were asked to discuss the decision they faced, how they were dealing with it, the alternatives they were considering, their reasons both for and against each option, the people involved, the conflicts entailed, and the ways in which making this decision affected their views of themselves and their relationships with others. In the second part of the interview, the women were asked to resolve three hypothetical moral dilemmas, including the Heinz dilemma from Kohlberg's research.

In extending Piaget's description of children's moral judgment to the moral judgment of adolescents and adults, Kohlberg (1976) distinguishes three perspectives on moral conflict and choice. Tying moral development in adolescence to the growth of reflective thought at that time, Kohlberg terms these three views of morality preconventional, conventional, and postconventional, to reflect the expansion in moral understanding from an individual to a societal to a universal point of view. In this scheme, conventional morality, or the equation of the right or good with the maintenance of existing social norms and values, is always the point of departure. Whereas preconventional moral judgment denotes an inability to construct a shared or societal viewpoint, postconventional judgment transcends that vision. Preconventional judgment is egocentric and derives moral constructs from individual needs; conventional judgment is based on the shared norms and values that sustain relationships, groups, communities, and societies; and postconventional judgment adopts a reflective perspective on societal values and constructs moral principles that are universal in application.

This shift in perspective toward increasingly differentiated, comprehensive, and reflective forms of thought appears in women's responses to both actual and hypothetical dilemmas. But just as the conventions that shape women's moral judgment differ from those that apply to men, so also women's definition of the moral domain diverges from that derived from studies of men. Women's construction of the moral problem as a problem of care and responsibility in relationships rather than as one of rights and rules ties the development of their moral thinking to changes in their understanding of responsibility and relationships, just as the conception of morality as justice ties development to the logic of equality and reciprocity. Thus the logic underlying an ethic of care is a psychological logic of relationships, which contrasts with the formal logic of fairness that informs the justice approach.

Women's constructions of the abortion dilemma in particular reveal the existence of a distinct moral language whose evolution traces a sequence of development. This is the language of selfishness and responsibility, which defines the moral problem as one of obligation to exercise care and avoid hurt. The inflicting of hurt is considered selfish and immoral in its reflection of unconcern, while the expression of care is seen as the fulfillment of moral responsibility. The reiterative use by the women of the words *selfish* and *responsible* in talking about moral conflict and choice, given the underlying moral orientation that this language reflects, sets the women apart from the men whom Kohlberg studied and points toward a different understanding of moral development.

The three moral perspectives revealed by the abortion decision study denote a sequence in the development of the ethic of care. These different views of care and the transitions between them emerged from an analysis of the ways in which the women used moral language—words such as *should, ought, better, right, good,* and *bad,* by the changes and shifts that appeared in their thinking, and by the way in which they reflected on and judged their thought. In this sequence, an initial focus on caring for the self in order to ensure survival is followed by a transitional phase in which this judgment is criticized as selfish. The criticism signals a new understanding of the connection between self and others which is articulated by the concept of responsibility. The elaboration of this concept of responsibility and its fusion with a maternal morality that seeks to ensure care for the dependent and unequal characterizes the second perspective. At this point, the good is equated with caring for others. However, when only others are legitimized as the recipients of the woman's care, the exclusion of herself gives rise to problems in relationships, creating a disequilibrium that initiates the second transition. The equation of conformity with care, in its conventional definition, and the illogic of the inequality between other and self, lead to a reconsideration of relationships in an effort to sort out the confusion between self-sacrifice and care inherent in the conventions of feminine goodness. The third perspective focuses on the dynamics of relationships and dissipates the tension between selfishness and responsibility through a new understanding of the interconnection between other and self. Care becomes the self-chosen principle of a judgment that remains psychological in its concern with relationships and response but becomes universal in its condemnation of exploitation and hurt. Thus a progressively more adequate understanding of the psychology of human relationships—an increasing differentiation of self and other and a growing comprehension of the dynamics of social interaction—informs the development of an ethic of care. This ethic, which reflects a cumulative knowledge of human relationships, evolves around a central insight, that self and other are interdependent. The different ways of thinking about this connection or the different modes of its apprehension mark the three perspectives and their transitional phases. In this sequence, the fact of interconnection informs the central, recurring recognition that just as the incidence of violence is in the end destructive to all, so the activity of care enhances both others and self.

In its simplest construction, the abortion decision centers on the self. The concern is pragmatic and the issue is survival. The woman focuses on taking care of herself because she feels that she is all alone. From this perspective, *should* is undifferentiated from *would*, and other people influence the decision only through their power to affect its consequences. Susan, an eighteen-year-old, asked what she thought when she found herself pregnant, replies: "I really didn't think anything except that I didn't want it. (*Why was that?*) I didn't want it, I wasn't ready for it, and next year will be my last year and I want to go to school." Asked if there is a right decision or a right way to decide about abortion, she says: "There is no right decision. (*Why?*) I didn't want it." For her, the question of rightness would emerge only if her own needs were in conflict; then she would have to decide which needs should take precedence. This is the dilemma of Joan, another eighteen-year-old, who sees having a baby not only as a way of increasing her freedom by providing "the perfect chance to get married and move away from home," but also as restricting her freedom "to do a lot of things."

In this mode of understanding, the self, which is the sole object of concern, is constrained by a lack of power that stems from feeling disconnected and thus, in effect, all alone. The wish "to do a lot of things" is constantly belied by the limitations of what has in fact been done. Relationships are for the most part disappointing: "The only thing you are ever going to get out of going with a guy is to get hurt." As a result, women in some instances deliberately choose isolation to protect themselves against hurt. When asked how she would describe herself, Martha, a nineteen-year-old who holds herself responsible for the accidental death of a younger brother to whom she felt particularly close, answers:

> I really don't know. I never thought about it. I don't know. I know basically the outline of a character. I am very independent. I don't really want to have to ask anybody for anything, and I am a loner in life. I prefer to be by myself than around anybody else. I manage to keep my friends at a limited number to the point that I have very few friends. I don't know what else there is. I am a loner, and I enjoy it. Here today and gone tomorrow.

The primacy of the concern with survival is explicitly acknowledged by Betty, a sixteen-year-old, in her judgment of Heinz's dilemma about stealing a drug to save the life of his wife:

I think survival is one of the first things in life that people fight for. I think it is the most important thing, more important than stealing. Stealing might be wrong, but if you have to steal to survive yourself or even kill, that is what you should do ... Preservation of oneself, I think, is the most important thing. It comes before anything in life.

In the transition that follows this position, the concepts of selfishness and responsibility first appear. Their reference initially is to the self, in a redefinition of the self-interest that has so far served as the basis for judgment. The transitional issue is one of attachment or connection to others. The pregnancy highlights this issue not only by representing an immediate, literal connection but also by affirming, in the most concrete and physical way, the capacity to assume adult feminine roles. Although having a baby at first seems to offer respite from the loneliness of adolescence and to solve conflicts over dependence and independence, in reality the continuation of an adolescent pregnancy generally compounds these problems, increasing social isolation and precluding further steps toward independence.

To be a mother in the societal as well as the physical sense requires the assumption of parental responsibility for the care and protection of a child. However, in order to be able to care for another, one must first be able to care responsibly for oneself. The growth from childhood to adulthood, conceived as a move from selfishness to responsibility, is articulated by Josie, a seventeen-year-old, in describing her response to pregnancy:

I started feeling really good about being pregnant instead of feeling really bad, because I wasn't looking at the situation realistically. I was looking at it from my own sort of selfish needs, because I was lonely. Things weren't really going good for me, so I was looking at it that I could have a baby that I could take care of or something that was part of me, and that made me feel good. But I wasn't looking at the realistic side, at the responsibility I would have to take on. I came to this decision that I was going to have an abortion because I realized how much responsibility goes with having a child. Like you have to be there; you can't be out of the house all the time, which is one thing I like to do. And I decided that I have to take on responsibility for myself and I have to work out a lot of things.

Describing her former mode of judgment, the wish to have a baby as a way of combating loneliness and making connection, Josie now criticizes that judgment as both "selfish" and "unrealistic." The contradiction between the wish for a baby and the wish for freedom to be "out of the house all the time"—that is, between connection and independence—is resolved in terms of a new priority. As the criterion for judgment shifts, the dilemma assumes a moral dimension, and the conflict between wish and necessity is cast as a disparity between "would" and "should." In this construction the "selfishness" of willful decision is counterposed to the "responsibility" of moral choice:

> What I want to do is to have the baby, but what I feel I should do, which is what I need to do, is have an abortion right now, because sometimes what you want isn't right. Sometimes what is necessary comes before what you want, because it might not always lead to the right thing.

Pregnancy itself confirms femininity, as Josie says: "I started feeling really good. Being pregnant, I started feeling like a woman." But the abortion decision becomes for her an opportunity for the adult exercise of responsible choice:

> (*How would you describe yourself to yourself?*) I am looking at myself differently in the way that I have had a really heavy decision put upon me, and I have never really had too many hard decisions in my life, and I have made it. It has taken some responsibility to do this. I have changed in that way, that I have made a hard decision. And that has been good. Because before, I would not have looked at it realistically, in my opinion. I would have gone by what I wanted to do, and I wanted it, and even if it wasn't right. So I see myself as becoming more mature in ways of making decisions and taking care of myself, doing something for myself. I think it is going to help me in other ways, if I have other decisions to make put upon me, which would take some responsibility. And I would know that I could make them.

In the epiphany of this cognitive reconstruction, the old becomes transformed in the new. The wish to "do something for myself" remains, but the terms of its fulfillment change. For Josie, the
abortion decision affirms both femininity and adulthood in its integration of care and responsibility. Morality, says another adolescent, "is the way you think about yourself. Sooner or later you
have to make up your mind to start taking care of yourself. Abortion, if you do it for the right reasons, is helping yourself to start
over and do different things."

Since this transition signals an enhancement in self-worth, it
requires a conception of self that includes the possibility for doing
"the right thing," the ability to see in oneself the potential for being
good and therefore worthy of social inclusion. When such confidence is seriously in doubt, the transitional issues may be raised,
but development is impeded. The failure to make this first transition, despite an understanding of the issues involved, is illustrated
by Anne, who in her late twenties struggles with the conflict between selfishness and responsibility but fails to resolve her dilemma
of whether or not to have a third abortion:

> I think you have to think about the people who are involved,
> including yourself. You have responsibilities to yourself. And
> to make a right—whatever that is—decision in this depends on
> your knowledge and awareness of the responsibilities that you
> have and whether you can survive with a child and what it
> will do to your relationship with the father or how it will af-
> fect him emotionally.

Rejecting the idea of selling the baby and making "a lot of
money in a black market kind of thing . . . because mostly I operate
on principles, and it would just rub me the wrong way to think I
would be selling my own child," Anne struggles with a concept of
responsibility which repeatedly turns back on the question of her
own survival. Transition seems blocked by a self-image that is insis-
tently contradictory:

> (*How would you describe yourself to yourself?*) I see myself as
> impulsive, practical—that is a contradiction—and moral and
> amoral, a contradiction. Acutally the only thing that is consis-
> tent and not contradictory is the fact that I am very lazy,
> which everyone has always told me is really a symptom of

something else which I have never been able to put my finger on exactly. It has taken me a long time to like myself. In fact, there are times when I don't, which I think is healthy to a point, and sometimes I think I like myself too much, and I probably evade myself too much, which avoids responsibility to myself and to other people who like me. I am pretty unfaithful to myself. I have a hard time even thinking that I am a human being, simply because so much rotten stuff goes on and people are so crummy and insensitive.

Seeing herself as avoiding responsibility, she can find no basis upon which to resolve the pregnancy dilemma. Her inability to arrive at any clear sense of decision only contributes further to her overall sense of failure. Criticizing her parents for having betrayed her during adolescence by coercing her into having an abortion she did not want, she now betrays herself and criticizes that as well. In this light, it is not surprising that she considers selling her child, since she feels herself to have, in effect, been sold by her parents for the sake of maintaining their reputation.

The transition from the first to the second perspective, the shift from selfishness to responsibility, is a move toward social participation. Whereas from the first perspective, morality is a matter of sanctions imposed by a society of which one is more subject than citizen, from the second perspective, moral judgment relies on shared norms and expectations. The woman at this point validates her claim to social membership through the adoption of societal values. Consensual judgment about goodness becomes the overriding concern as survival is now seen to depend on acceptance by others.

Here the conventional feminine voice emerges with great clarity, defining the self and proclaiming its worth on the basis of the ability to care for and protect others. The woman now constructs a world perfused with the assumptions about feminine goodness that are reflected in the stereotypes of the Broverman et al. studies (1972), where all the attributes considered desirable for women presume an other—the recipient of the "tact, gentleness and easy expression of feeling" which allow the woman to respond sensitively while evoking in return the care that meets her "very strong need for security" (p. 63). The strength of this position lies in its capacity for caring; the limitation of this position lies in the restriction it imposes on direct expression. Both qualities are elucidated by

Judy, a nineteen-year-old who contrasts her own reluctance to criticize with her boyfriend's straightforwardness:

> I never want to hurt anyone, and I tell them in a very nice way, and I have respect for their own opinions, and they can do things the way that they want. He usually tells people right off the bat. He does a lot of things out in public which I do in private. It is better, but I just could never do it.

While her judgment clearly exists, it is not expressed, at least not in public. Concern for the feelings of others imposes a deference to them which she nevertheless criticizes in her awareness that, under the name of consideration, a vulnerability and a duplicity are concealed.

At this point in development, conflict arises specifically over the issue of hurting. When no option exists that can be construed as being in the best interest of everybody, when responsibilities conflict and decision entails the sacrifice of somebody's needs, then the woman confronts the seemingly impossible task of choosing the victim. Cathy, a nineteen-year-old, fearing the consequences for herself of a second abortion, but facing opposition from both her family and her lover to the continuation of the pregnancy, describes the dilemma:

> I don't know what choices are open to me. It is either to have it or the abortion; these are the choices open to me. I think what confuses me is it is a choice of either hurting myself or hurting other people around me. What is more important? If there could be a happy medium, it would be fine, but there isn't. It is either hurting someone on this side or hurting myself.

Although the feminine identification of goodness with self-sacrifice clearly dictates the "right" resolution of this dilemma, the stakes may be high for the woman herself, and in any event the sacrifice of the fetus compromises the altruism of an abortion motivated by concern for others. Since femininity itself is in conflict in an abortion intended as an expression of love and care, this resolution readily explodes in its own contradiction.

"I don't think anyone should have to choose between two things that they love," says Denise, a twenty-five-year-old who had an abortion she did not want because she felt a responsibility not only for her lover but also for his wife and children:

> I just wanted the child, and I really don't believe in abortions. Who can say when life begins? I think that life begins at conception. I felt like there were changes happening in my body, and I felt very protective. But I felt a responsibility, my responsibility if anything ever happened to [his wife]. He made me feel that I had to make a choice and there was only one choice to make and that was to have an abortion and I could always have children another time, and he made me feel if I didn't have it that it would drive us apart.

The abortion decision was in her mind a choice not to choose with respect to the pregnancy: "That was my choice: I had to do it." Instead, she chose to subordinate the pregnancy to the continuation of a relationship that she saw as encompassing her life: "Since I met him, he has been my life. I do everything for him; my life sort of revolves around him." Since she wanted to have the baby and also wanted to continue the relationship, either choice could be construed as selfish. Furthermore, since both alternatives entailed hurting someone, neither could be considered moral. Faced with a decision which, in her own terms, was untenable, she sought to avoid responsibility for the choice she made, construing the decision as a sacrifice of her own needs to those of her lover and his wife. However, this public sacrifice in the name of responsibility engendered a private resentment that erupted in anger, compromising the very relationship it was intended to sustain:

> Afterwards we went through a bad time because—I hate to say it and I was wrong—but I blamed him. I gave in to him. But when it came down to it, I made the decision. I could have said, "I am going to have this child, whether you want me to or not," and I just didn't do it.

Pregnant again by the same man, she recognizes in retrospect that the choice was in fact hers, as she returns once again to what now appears to have been a missed opportunity for growth. Seeking this time to make rather than abdicate the decision, she sees the issue as one of "strength," and she struggles to free herself from the powerlessness of her own dependence:

Right now I think of myself as someone who can become a lot stronger. Because of the circumstances, I just go along with the tide. I never really had anything of my own before ... I hope to come on strong and make a big decision, whether it is right or wrong.

Because the morality of self-sacrifice justified the previous abortion, she now must suspend that judgment if she is to claim her own voice and accept responsibility for choice. She thereby calls into question the assumption underlying her former perspective, that she is responsible for the actions of others while others are responsible for the choices she makes. This notion of responsibility, backwards in its assumptions about control, disguises assertion as response. By reversing responsibility, it generates a series of indirect actions, which in the end leave everyone feeling manipulated and betrayed. The logic of this position is confused in that the morality of mutual care is embedded in the psychology of dependence. Assertion becomes potentially immoral in its power to hurt. This confusion is captured in Kohlberg's definition of the third stage of moral development which joins the need for approval with the wish to care for and help others. When thus caught between the passivity of dependence and the activity of care, the woman becomes suspended in a paralysis of initiative with respect to both action and thought. Thus Denise speaks of herself as "just going along with the tide."

The transitional phase that follows this judgment is marked by a shift in concern from goodness to truth. The transition begins with reconsideration of the relationship between self and other, as the woman starts to scrutinize the logic of self-sacrifice in the service of a morality of care. In the abortion interviews this transition is announced by the reappearance of the word *selfish*. Retrieving the judgmental initiative, the woman begins to ask whether it is selfish or responsible, moral or immoral, to include her own needs within the compass of her care and concern. This question leads her to reexamine the concept of responsibility, juxtaposing the concern with what other people think with a new inner judgment.

In separating the voice of the self from the voices of others, the woman asks if it is possible to be responsible to herself as well as to others and thus to reconcile the disparity between hurt and care. The exercise of such responsibility requires a new kind of judgment, whose first demand is for honesty. To be responsible for oneself, it is first necessary to acknowledge what one is doing. The criterion for judgment thus shifts from goodness to truth when the morality of action is assessed not on the basis of its appearance in the eyes of others, but in terms of the realities of its intention and consequence.

Janet, a twenty-four-year-old married Catholic, pregnant again two months following the birth of her first child, identifies her dilemma as one of choice: "You have to decide now. Because abortion is now available, you have to make a decision. And if it weren't available, there would be no choice open; you just do what you have to do." In the absence of legal abortion, a morality of self-sacrifice is necessary in order to ensure protection and care for the dependent child. However, when such sacrifice becomes optional, the entire problem is recast.

The abortion decision is framed by Janet first in terms of her responsibilities to others, since having a second child at this time would be contrary to medical advice and would strain both the emotional and financial resources of the family. However, there is, she says, another reason for having an abortion, "sort of an emotional reason. I don't know if it is selfish or not, but it would really be tying myself down, and right now I am not ready to be tied down with two."

Against this combination of selfish and responsible reasons for abortion is her religious belief about abortion:

> It is taking a life. Even though it is not formed, it is the potential, and to me it is still taking a life. But I have to think of mine, my son's, and my husband's. And at first I thought it was for selfish reasons, but it is not. I believe that, too, some of it is selfish. I don't want another one right now; I am not ready for it."

The dilemma arises over the issue of justification for taking a life. "I can't cover it over, because I believe this, and if I do try to cover it over, I know that I am going to be in a mess. It will be denying what I am really doing." Asking herself, "Am I doing the right thing; is it moral?" Janet counterposes her beliefs about abortion to her concern with the consequences of continuing the pregnancy. Concluding that she cannot be "so morally strict as to hurt three other people with a decision just because of my moral beliefs," she finds that the issue of goodness still remains critical to her resolution of the dilemma:

> The moral factor is there. To me it is taking a life, and I am going to take that decision upon myself, and I have feelings about it, and talked to a priest. But he said it is there, and it will be from now on, and it is up to the person if they can live with the idea and still believe they are good.

The criteria for goodness, however, move inward since the ability to have an abortion and still consider herself good hinges on the issue of selfishness. Asked if acting morally is acting according to what is best for the self or whether it is a matter of self-sacrifice, she replies:

> I don't know if I really understand the question. In my situation, where I want to have the abortion, and if I didn't it would be self-sacrificing, I am really in the middle of both those ways. But I think that my morality is strong, and if these reasons—financial, physical reality, and also for the whole family involved—were not here, that I wouldn't have to do it, and then it would be a self-sacrifice.

The importance of clarifying her own participation in the decision is evident in her attempt to ascertain her feelings in order to determine whether or not she is "putting them under" in deciding to end the pregnancy. In the first transition, from selfishness to responsibility, women make lists in order to bring to their consideration needs other than their own. But in the second transition, from goodness to truth, the needs of the self have to be deliberately uncovered. Confronting the reality of her own wish for an abortion, Janet deals with the problem of selfishness and the qualification that it seems to impose on the "goodness" of her decision. But the concern with selfishness yields in the end to a concern with honesty and truth:

> I think in a way I am selfish, and very emotional, and I think that I am a very real person and an understanding person, and I can handle life situations fairly well, so I am basing a lot of it on my ability to do the things that I feel are right and best

for me and whomever I am involved with. I think I was very fair to myself about the decision, and I really think that I have been truthful, not hiding anything, bringing out all the feelings involved. I feel it is a good decision and an honest one, a real decision.

Thus she strives to encompass the needs of both self and others, to be responsible to others and thus to be "good" but also to be responsible to herself and thus to be "honest" and "real."

Although from one point of view, paying attention to one's own needs is selfish, from a different perspective it is not only honest but fair. This is the essence of the transitional shift toward a new concept of goodness, which turns inward in acknowledging the self and in accepting responsibility for choice. Outward justification, the concern with "good reasons," remains critical for Janet: "I still think abortion is wrong, and it will be unless the situation can justify what you are doing." However, the search for justification produces a change in her thinking, "not drastically, but a little bit." She realizes that in continuing the pregnancy, she would punish not only herself but also her husband, toward whom she has begun to feel "turned off and irritated." This leads her to consider the possible consequences of self-sacrifice both for the self and for others. At the end, Janet says, "God can punish, but He can also forgive." What remains in question for her is whether her claim to forgiveness is compromised by a decision that not only meets the needs of others but also is "right and best for me."

The concern with selfishness and its equation with immorality recur in an interview with Sandra, a twenty-nine-year-old Catholic nurse, who punctuates her arrival for an abortion with the statement, "I have always thought abortion was a fancy word for murder." Initially she explains this murder as one of lesser degree, because "I am doing it because I have to do it. I am not doing it the least bit because I want to." Thus, she judges it "not quite as bad. You can rationalize that it is not quite the same." Since "keeping the child for lots and lots of reasons was just sort of impractical and out," she considers her options to be either abortion or adoption. Having previously given up one child for adoption, she finds that "psychologically there was no way that I could hack another adoption. It took me about four and a half years to get my head on straight. There was just no way I was going to go through it again." The decision thus reduces in her eyes to a choice between mur-

dering the fetus or damaging herself. The choice is further complicated by the fact that to continue the pregnancy would hurt not
only herself but also her parents, with whom she lives. In the face
of these manifold moral contradictions, the psychological honesty
demanded in counseling finally allows her to reach a decision:

> On my own, I was doing it not so much for myself; I was
> doing it for my parents. I was doing it because the doctor told
> me to do it, but I had never resolved in my mind that I was
> doing it for me. Actually, I had to sit down and admit, "No, I
> really don't want to go the mother route now. I honestly don't
> feel that I want to be a mother." And that is not really such a
> bad thing to say after all. But that is not how I felt up until
> talking to [her counselor]. It was just a horrible way to feel, so
> I just wasn't going to feel it, and I just blocked it right out.

As long as her consideration remains "moral," abortion can be
justified only as an act of sacrifice, a submission to necessity where
the absence of choice precludes responsibility. In this way, she can
avoid self-condemnation, since, "When you get into moral stuff,
then you are getting into self-respect, and if I do something that I
feel is morally wrong, then I tend to lose some of my self-respect as
a person." Her evasion of responsibility, critical to maintaining the
innocence she considers necessary for self-respect, contradicts the
reality of her participation in the abortion decision. The dishonesty
in her plea of victimization creates a conflict that generates the
need for a more inclusive understanding. She must now resolve the
emerging contradiction in her thinking between her two uses of the
terms *right* and *wrong*: "I am saying that abortion is morally wrong,
but the situation is right, and I am going to do it. But the thing is
that eventually they are going to have to go together, and I am
going to have to put them together somehow." Asked how this
could be done, she replies:

> I would have to change morally wrong to morally right.
> (*How?*) I have no idea. I don't think you can take something
> that you feel is morally wrong because the situation makes it
> right and put the two together. They are not together, they are
> opposite. They don't go together. Something is wrong, but all
> of a sudden, because you are doing it, it is right.

This discrepancy recalls a similar conflict she faced over the question of euthanasia, which she also considered morally wrong until she was responsible for the care of "a couple of patients who had flat EEGs and saw the job that it was doing on their families." That experience led her to realize:

> You really don't know your black and whites until you really get into them and are being confronted with it. If you stop and think about my feelings on euthanasia until I got into it, and then my feelings about abortion until I got into it, I thought both of them were murder. Right and wrong and no middle, but there is a gray.

In discovering the gray and questioning the moral judgments that formerly she considered absolute, she confronts the moral crisis of the second transition. Now the conventions which in the past guided her moral judgment become subject to a new criticism, as she questions not only the justification for hurting others in the name of morality but also the "rightness" of hurting herself. However, to sustain such criticism in the face of conventions that equate goodness with self-sacrifice, Sandra must verify her capacity for independent judgment and the legitimacy of her own point of view.

Once again transition hinges on self-concept. When uncertainty about her own worth prevents a woman from claiming equality, self-assertion falls prey to the old criticism of selfishness. Then the morality that condones self-destruction in the name of responsible care is not repudiated as inadequate but is rather abandoned in the face of its threat to survival. Moral obligation, rather than expanding to include the self, is rejected completely when the failure of response leaves the woman unwilling any longer to protect others at what is now seen to be her own expense. In the absence of morality, survival, however "selfish" or "immoral," returns as the paramount concern.

Ellen, a musician in her late twenties, illustrates this transitional impasse. Having led an independent life that centered on her work, she considered herself "fairly strong-willed, fairly in control, fairly rational and objective," until she became involved in an intense love affair and discovered in her capacity to love an "entirely new dimension" in herself. Admitting in retrospect to "tremendous naiveté and idealism," she had entertained "vague ideas that some day I would like a child to concretize our relationship, having always associated having a child with all the creative aspects of my life." Abjuring, with her lover, the use of contraceptives because, "as the relationship was sort of an ideal relationship in our minds, we liked the idea of not using foreign objects or anything artificial," she saw herself as having relinquished control, becoming instead "just simply vague and allowing events to just carry me along." When she began to confront "the realities of that situation"—the possibility of pregnancy and the fact that her lover was married—she found that she was pregnant. "Caught" between her wish to end a relationship that "seemed more and more defeating" and her wish for a baby, which "would be a connection that would last a long time," she is paralyzed by her inability to resolve the dilemma that her ambivalence creates.

The pregnancy poses a conflict between her "moral" belief that "once a certain life has begun, it shouldn't be stopped artificially," and her "amazing" discovery that, to have the baby, she would need much more support than she had thought. Despite her moral conviction that she "should" have the child, she doubts that she can psychologically deal with "having the child alone and taking the responsibility for it." Thus a conflict erupts between what she considers to be her moral obligation to protect life and her inability to do so under the circumstances of this pregnancy. Seeing it as "my decision and my responsibility for making the decision whether to have or have not the child," she struggles to find a viable basis on which to resolve the dilemma.

Capable of arguing either for or against abortion "with a philosophical logic," Ellen thinks, on the one hand, that in an overpopulated world one should have children only under ideal conditions for care, but on the other, that one should end a life only when it is impossible to sustain it. Asked whether there is a difference between what she wants to do and what she thinks she should do, she describes the impasse that she has recurrently faced:

Yes, and there always has been. I have always been confronted with that precise situation in a lot of my choices, and I have been trying to figure out what are the things that make me believe that these are things I should do as opposed to what I feel I want to do. (*In this situation?*) It is not that clearcut. I both want the child and feel I should have it, and I also think I should have the abortion and want it, but I would say it is my stronger feeling. I don't have enough confidence in my work yet, and that is really where it is all hinged. The abortion would solve the problem, and I know I can't handle the pregnancy.

Characterizing abortion as an "emotional and pragmatic" solution and attributing it to her lack of confidence in her work, she contrasts this solution with the "better thought-out and more logical and more correct" resolution of her lover, who thinks she should have the child and raise it without either his presence or his financial support. Confronted with this reflected image of herself as ultimately giving and good, as self-sustaining in her own creativity and thus able to meet the needs of a baby while imposing no demands on others, Ellen questions not the image itself but her own adequacy to fill it. Concluding that she is not yet capable of doing so, she is reduced in her own eyes to what she sees as a selfish and highly compromised fight "for my survival." But she says:

> In one way or another I am going to suffer. Maybe I am going to suffer mentally and emotionally having the abortion, or I would suffer what I think is possibly something worse. So I suppose it is the lesser of two evils. I think it is a matter of choosing which one I know that I can survive through. It is really. I think it is selfish, I suppose, because it does have to do with that. I just realized that. I guess it does have to do with whether I would survive or not. (*Why is this selfish?*) Well, you know, it is. Because I am concerned with my survival first, as opposed to the survival of the relationship or the survival of the child, another human being. I guess I am setting priorities, and I guess I am setting my needs to survive first. I guess I see it in negative terms a lot. But I do think of other positive things, that I am still going to have some life left, maybe. I don't know.

In the face of this failure of care, in the disappointment of abandonment where connection was sought, Ellen considers survival to hinge on her work, which is "where I derive the meaning of what I am. That's the known factor." Although uncertainty about her work makes this survival precarious, the choice of abortion is also precarious in that it is "highly introverted." Having an abortion "would be going a step backward," whereas "going outside to love someone else and having a child would be a step forward." The sense of retrenchment that the severing of connection signifies is apparent in her anticipation of the cost that abortion will entail:

> Probably what I will do is I will cut off my feelings, and when they will return or what would happen to them after that, I don't know. So that I don't feel anything at all, and I would probably just be very cold and go through it very coldly. The more you do that to yourself, the more difficult it becomes to love again or to trust again or to feel again. Each time I move away from that, it becomes easier, not more difficult, but easier to avoid committing myself to a relationship. And I am really concerned about cutting off that whole feeling aspect.

Caught between selfishness and responsibility, unable to find in the circumstances of this choice a way of caring that does not at the same time destroy, Ellen confronts a dilemma that reduces to a conflict between morality and survival. Adulthood and femininity fly apart in the failure of this attempt at integration, as the choice to work becomes a decision not only to renounce this particular relationship and child but also to obliterate the vulnerability that love and care engender.

But the problems in this understanding give rise to the insight of the third perspective, as the focus shifts to the consideration of what constitutes care. Sarah, a twenty-five-year-old who also faces disappointment, finds a way to reconcile the initially disparate concepts of selfishness and responsibility through a transformed understanding of relationships. Examining the assumptions underlying the conventions of female self-abnegation and moral self-sacrifice, she rejects these conventions as immoral in their power to hurt. By elevating nonviolence, the injunction against hurting, to a principle governing all moral judgment and action, she is able to assert a moral equality between self and other and to include both in the compass of care. Care then becomes a universal injunction, a self-chosen ethic which, freed from its conventional interpretation, leads to a recasting of the dilemma in a way that allows the assumption of responsibility for choice.

In Sarah's life, the current pregnancy brings to the surface the unfinished business of an earlier pregnancy and of the relationship in which both pregnancies occurred. Sarah had discovered the first pregnancy after her lover left her, and she terminated it by an abortion which she experienced as a purging expression of her anger at having been rejected. Remembering the abortion only as a relief, she nevertheless describes that time in her life as one in which she "hit rock bottom." Having hoped to "take control of my life," she instead resumed the relationship when the man reappeared. Two years later, having once again "left my diaphragm in the drawer," she again became pregnant. Although initially "ecstatic" at the news, her elation dissipated when her lover told her that he would leave if she chose to have the child. Under these circumstances she considered a second abortion but was unable to keep the repeated appointments she made because of her reluctance to accept the responsibility for that choice. While the first abortion seemed an "honest mistake," a second one would make her feel "like a walking slaughter-house." Since she would need financial support to raise the child, her initial strategy was to take the matter to "the welfare people" in the hope that they would refuse to provide the necessary funds and thus resolve her dilemma:

> In that way, you know, the responsibility would be off my shoulders, and I could say, "It's not my fault. The state denied me the money that I would need to do it." But it turned out that it was possible to do it, and so I was, you know, right back where I started. And I had an appointment for an abortion, and I kept calling and canceling it, and then remaking the appointment and canceling it, and I just couldn't make up my mind.

Confronting a choice between the two evils of hurting herself or ending the incipient life of the child, Sarah reconstructs the dilemma in a way that yields a new priority which allows decision. In doing so, she comes to see the conflict as arising from a faulty construction of reality. She recapitulates the sequence of development as she first considers, but then rejects as inadequate, resolutions based on her feelings of loneliness or her wish to appear good in others' eyes. In the end, she subsumes these considerations to concerns about responsibility for herself as well as for the father and the child:

> Well, the pros for having the baby are all the admiration that you would get from being a single woman, alone, martyr, struggling, having the adoring love of this beautiful Gerber

baby. Just more of a home life than I have had in a long time, and that basically was it, which is pretty fantasyland. It is not very realistic. Cons against having the baby: it was going to hasten what is looking to be the inevitable end of the relationship with the man I am presently with. I was going to have to go on welfare. My parents were going to hate me for the rest of my life. I was going to lose a really good job that I have. I would lose a lot of independence. Solitude. And I would have to be put in a position of asking help from a lot of people a lot of the time. Con against having the abortion is having to face up to the guilt. And pros for having the abortion are I would be able to handle my deteriorating relation with [the father] with a lot more capability and a lot more responsibility for him and for myself. I would not have to go through the realization that for the next twenty-five years of my life I would be punishing myself for being foolish enough to get pregnant again and forcing myself to bring up a kid just because I did this. Having to face the guilt of a second abortion seemed like not exactly—well, exactly the lesser of the two evils, but also the one that would pay off for me personally in the long run because, by looking at why I am pregnant again and subsequently have decided to have a second abortion, I have to face up to some things about myself.

Although Sarah does not "feel good" about having a second abortion, she concludes:

I would not be doing myself or the child or the world any kind of favor having this child. I don't need to pay off my imaginary debts to the world through this child, and I don't think that it is right to bring a child into the world and use it for that purpose.

Asked to describe herself, she indicates how closely her transformed moral understanding is tied to a changing self-concept:

1 have been thinking about that a lot lately, and it comes up different than what my usual subconscious perception of myself is. Usually paying off some sort of debt, going around serving people who are not really worthy of my attention, because somewhere in life I think I got the impression that my

needs are really secondary to other people's, and that if I feel, if I make any demands on other people to fulfill my needs, I'd feel guilty for it and submerge my own in favor of other people's, which later backfires on me, and I feel a great deal of resentment for other people that I am doing things for, which causes friction and the eventual deterioration of the relationship. And then I start all over again. How would I describe myself to myself? Pretty frustrated and a lot angrier than I admit, a lot more aggressive than I admit.

Reflecting on the virtues which comprise the conventional definition of the feminine self, a definition that she hears articulated in her mother's voice, she says, "I am beginning to think that all these virtues are really not getting me anywhere. I have begun to notice." Tied to this recognition is an acknowledgment of her own power and worth, both of which were excluded from the image she previously projected:

> I am suddenly beginning to realize that the things that I like to do, the things I am interested in, and the things that I believe and the kind of person I am, are not so bad that I have to constantly be sitting on the shelf and letting it gather dust. I am a lot more worthwhile than my past actions have led other people to believe.

Sarah's notion of a "good person," which previously was limited to her mother's example of hard work, patience, and self-sacrifice, changes to include the value that she herself places on directness and honesty. Although she believes that this new self-assertion will lead her to "feel a lot better about myself," she recognizes that it will also expose her to criticism:

> Other people may say, "Boy, she's aggressive, and I don't like that," but at least they will know that they don't like that. They are not going to say, "I like the way she manipulates herself to fit right around me." What I want to do is just be a more self-determined person and a more singular person.

Within her old framework, abortion seemed a way of "copping out," saving her from being a responsible person who "pays for her mistakes, and pays and pays, and is always there when she says she will be there, and even when she doesn't say she will be there is there." Within the new framework, her conception of herself and of what is "right for myself" is changing. She can consider this emergent self "a good person" because her concept of goodness has expanded to encompass the feeling of "self-worth," the feeling that "you are not going to sell yourself short and you are not going to make yourself do things that you know are really stupid and that you don't want to do." This reorientation centers on a new awareness of responsibility:

> I have this responsibility to myself, and you know, for once I am beginning to realize that that really matters to me. Instead of doing what I want for myself and feeling guilty over how selfish I am, you realize that that is a very usual way for people to live—doing what you want to do because you feel that your wants and your needs are important, if to no one else, then to you, and that's reason enough to do something that you want to do.

Once obligation extends to include the self as well as others, the disparity between selfishness and responsibility dissolves. Although the conflict between self and other remains, the moral problem is reconstructed in light of the realization that the occurrence of the dilemma itself precludes nonviolent resolution. The abortion decision comes to be seen as a "serious" choice affecting both self and others: "This is a life that I have taken, a conscious decision to terminate, and that is just very heavy, a very heavy thing." While accepting the necessity of abortion as a highly compromised resolution, Sarah turns her attention to the pregnancy itself, which to her denotes a failure of responsibility, a failure to care for and protect both other and self.

As in the first transition, although now in different terms, the conflict precipitated by the pregnancy catches up issues that are critical to psychological development. These issues pertain to the worth of the self in relation to others, the claiming of the power to choose, and the acceptance of responsibility for choice. By provoking a confrontation with choice, the abortion crisis can become a "very auspicious time. You can use the pregnancy as sort of a learning, a teeing-off point, which makes it useful in a way." The same sense of a possibility for growth in this crisis is expressed by other women, who arrive through this encounter with choice at a new understanding of relationships and speak of their sense of "a new beginning," a chance "to take control of my life."

For Sarah, facing a second abortion, the first step in taking control is to end the relationship in which she has considered herself "reduced to a nonentity," but to do so in a responsible way. Recognizing hurt as the inevitable concomitant of rejection, she strives to minimize that hurt by dealing with her lover's needs "as best I can without compromising my own. That's a big point for me, because the thing in my life to this point has always been compromising, and I am not willing to do that any more." Instead, she seeks to act in a "decent, human kind of way, one that leaves maybe a slightly shaken but not totally destroyed person." Thus the "nonentity" confronts her power to destroy, which formerly had impeded assertion, and considers the possibility for a new kind of action that leaves both self and other intact.

The moral concern remains a concern with hurting as Sarah considers Heinz's dilemma in terms of the question, "Who is going to be hurt more, the druggist who loses some money or the person who loses her life?" The right to property and the right to life are weighed not in the abstract, in terms of their logical priority, but in the particular, in terms of the actual consequences that the violation of these rights will have in the lives of the people involved. Sarah's thinking remains contextual and admixed with feelings of care, but the moral imperative to avoid hurt begins to be informed by a more complex understanding of the psychological dynamics of relationships.

Thus, release from the intimidation of inequality finally allows women to express a judgment that had previously been withheld. What women then enunciate is not a new morality, but a morality disentangled from the constraints that formerly confused its perception and impeded its articulation. The willingness to express and to take responsibility for judgment stems from a recognition of the psychological costs of indirect action, to self and to others and thus to relationships. Responsibility for care then includes both self and other, and the injunction not to hurt, freed from conventional constraints, sustains the ideal of care while focusing the reality of choice.

The reality of hurt centers the judgment of Ruth, a twenty-nine-year-old married woman and the mother of a preschool child, as she struggles with the dilemma posed by a second pregnancy whose timing conflicts with her completion of an advanced degree.

Saying that she "cannot deliberately do something that is bad or would hurt another person because I can't live with having done that," she nevertheless confronts a situation in which hurt has become inevitable. Seeking the solution that best protects both herself and others, she defines morality in a way that combines the recognition of interconnection between self and others with an awareness of the self as the arbiter of moral judgment and choice:

> Morality is doing what is appropriate and what is just within your circumstances, but ideally it is not going to affect—I was going to say, "ideally it wouldn't negatively affect another person," but that is ridiculous, because decisions are always going to affect another person. But what I am trying to say is that it is the person that is the center of the decision-making about what's right and what's wrong.

The person who is at the center of this particular decision about abortion begins by denying, but goes on to acknowledge, the conflicting nature both of her own needs and of her various responsibilities. Seeing the pregnancy as a manifestation of the inner conflict between her wish, on the one hand, "to be a college president" and, on the other, "to be making pottery and flowers and having kids and staying at home," Ruth struggles with the contradiction between femininity and adulthood. Considering abortion as the "better" choice, because "in the end, meaning this time next year or this time two weeks from now, it will be less of a personal strain on us individually and on us as a family for me not to be pregnant at this time," she concludes:

> The decision has got to be, first of all, something that the woman can live with, a decision that the woman can live with, one way or another, or at least try to live with, and it must be based on where she is at and other significant people in her life are at.

At the beginning of the interview Ruth presents the abortion dilemma in its conventional feminine construction, as a conflict between her own wish to have a baby and the wish of others to have her complete her education. On the basis of this construction she deems it "selfish" to continue the pregnancy because it is something

"I want to do." However, as she begins to examine her thinking, she abandons as false this conceptualization of the problem, acknowledging the truth of her own internal conflict and elaborating the tension she feels between her femininity and the adulthood of her work life. She describes herself as "going in two directions" and values that part of herself which is "incredibly passionate and sensitive," her capacity to recognize and meet the needs of others. Seeing her "compassion" as "something I don't want to lose," she regards it as endangered by her pursuit of professional advancement. Thus the self-deception of her initial presentation, its attempt to sustain the fiction of her innocence, stems from her fear of what saying that she does not want to have another baby at this time would mean:

> It would be an acknowledgment to me that I am an ambitious person and that I want to have power and responsibility for others and that I want to live a life that extends from 9 to 5 every day and into the evenings and on weekends, because that is what the power and responsibility mean. It means that my family would necessarily come second. There would be such an incredible conflict about which is tops, and I don't want that for myself.

Asked about her concept of "an ambitious person," she says:

> To be ambitious means to be power hungry and insensitive. (*Why insensitive?*) Because people are stomped on in the process. A person on the way up stomps on people, whether it is family or other colleagues or clientele. (*Inevitably?*) Not always, but I have seen it so often in my limited years of working that it is scary to me. It is scary because I don't want to change like that.

Because Ruth sees the acquisition of adult power as entailing the loss of feminine sensitivity and compassion, she construes the conflict between femininity and adulthood as a moral problem. The abortion dilemma then directs her attention to what it means in this society to be a woman and to be an adult, and the recognition of the disparity between power and care initiates the search for a resolution that can encompass both femininity and adulthood, in relationships and at work.

To admit the truth of the women's perspective to the conception of moral development is to recognize for both sexes the importance throughout life of the connection between self and other, the universality of the need for compassion and care. The concept of the separate self and of moral principles uncompromised by the constraints of reality is an adolescent ideal, the elaborately wrought philosophy of a Stephen Daedalus whose flight we know to be in jeopardy. Erikson (1964), in contrasting the ideological morality of the adolescent with the adult ethic of taking care, attempts to grapple with this problem of integration. But when he charts a developmental path where the sole precursor to the intimacy of adult love and the generativity of adult work and relationships is the trust established in infancy, and where all intervening experience is marked as steps toward autonomy and independence, then separation itself becomes the model and the measure of growth. Though Erikson observes that, for women, identity has as much to do with intimacy as with separation, this observation is not integrated into his developmental chart.

The morality of responsibility that women describe stands, like their concept of self, apart from the path marked to maturity. The progress to moral maturity is depicted as leading through the adolescent questioning of conventional morality to the discovery of individual rights. The generalization of this discovery into a principled conception of justice is illustrated by the definition of morality given by Ned, a senior in the college student study:

> Morality is a prescription, a thing to follow, and the idea of having a concept of morality is to try to figure out what it is that people can do in order to make life with each other livable, make for a kind of balance, a kind of equilibrium, a harmony in which everybody feels he has a place and an equal share in things. Doing that is kind of contributing to a state of affairs that goes beyond the individual, in the absence of whch the individual has no chance for self-fulfillment of any kind. Fairness, morality, is kind of essential, it seems to me, for creating the kind of environment, interaction between people, that is prerequisite to the fulfillment of most individual goals. If you want other people not to interfere with your pursuit of whatever you are into, you have to play the game.

In contrast, Diane, a woman in her late twenties, defines a morality not of rights but of responsibility, when explaining what makes an issue moral:

> Some sense of trying to uncover a right path in which to live, and always in my mind is that the world is full of real and recognizable trouble, and it is heading for some sort of doom, and is it right to bring children into this world when we currently have an overpopulation problem, and is it right to spend money on a pair of shoes when I have a pair of shoes and other people are shoeless? It is part of a self-critical view, part of saying, "How am I spending my time and in what sense am I working?" I think I have a real drive, a real maternal drive, to take care of someone—to take care of my mother, to take care of children, to take care of other people's children, to take care of my own children, to take care of the world. When I am dealing with moral issues, I am sort of saying to myself constantly, "Are you taking care of all the things that you think are important, and in what ways are you wasting yourself and wasting those issues?"

While the postconventional nature of Diane's perspective seems clear, her judgment of moral dilemmas does not meet the criteria for principled thinking in the justice orientation. This judgment, however, reflects a different moral conception in which moral judgment is oriented toward issues of responsibility and care. The way in which the responsibility orientation guides moral decision at the postconventional level is illustrated by Sharon, a woman in her thirties when questioned about the right way to make moral decisions:

> The only way I know is to try to be as awake as possible, to try to know the range of what you feel, to try to consider all that's involved, to be as aware as you can be of what's going on, as conscious as you can of where you're walking. (*Are there principles that guide you?*) The principle would have something to do with responsibility, responsibility and caring about yourself and others. But it's not that on the one hand you choose to be responsible and on the other hand you choose to be irresponsible. Both ways you can be responsible. That's why there's not just a principle that once you take hold

of you settle. The principle put into practice here is still going to leave you with conflict.

The moral imperative that emerges repeatedly in interviews with women is an injunction to care, a responsibility to discern and alleviate the "real and recognizable trouble" of this world. For men, the moral imperative appears rather as an injunction to respect the rights of others and thus to protect from interference the rights to life and self-fulfillment. Women's insistence on care is at first self-critical rather than self-protective, while men initially conceive obligation to others negatively in terms of noninterference. Development for both sexes would therefore seem to entail an integration of rights and responsibilities through the discovery of the complementarity of these disparate views. For women, the integration of rights and responsibilities takes place through an understanding of the psychological logic of relationships. This understanding tempers the self-destructive potential of a self-critical morality by asserting the need of all persons for care. For men, recognition through experience of the need for more active responsibility in taking care corrects the potential indifference of a morality of noninterference and turns attention from the logic to the consequences of choice (Gilligan and Murphy, 1979; Gilligan, 1981). In the development of a postconventional ethical understanding, women come to see the violence inherent in inequality, while men come to see the limitations of a conception of justice blinded to the differences in human life.

Hypothetical dilemmas, in the abstraction of their presentation, divest moral actors from the history and psychology of their individual lives and separate the moral problem from the social contingencies of its possible occurrence. In doing so, these dilemmas are useful for the distillation and refinement of objective principles of justice and for measuring the formal logic of equality and reciprocity. However, the reconstruction of the dilemma in its contextual particularity allows the understanding of cause and consequence which engages the compassion and tolerance repeatedly noted to distinguish the moral judgments of women. Only when substance is given to the skeletal lives of hypothetical people is it possible to consider the social injustice that their moral problems may reflect and to imagine the individual suffering their occurrence may signify or their resolution engender.

The proclivity of women to reconstruct hypothetical dilemmas in terms of the real, to request or to supply missing information about the nature of the people and the places where they live, shifts their judgment away from the hierarchical ordering of principles and the formal procedures of decision making. This insistence on the particular signifies an orientation to the dilemma and to moral problems in general that differs from any current developmental stage descriptions. Consequently, though several of the women in the abortion study clearly articulate a postconventional metaethical position, none of them are considered principled in their normative moral judgments of Kohlberg's hypothetical dilemmas. Instead, the women's judgments point toward an identification of the violence inherent in the dilemma itself, which is seen to compromise the justice of any of its possible resolutions. This construction of the dilemma leads the women to recast the moral judgment from a consideration of the good to a choice between evils.

Ruth, the woman who spoke of her conflicting wishes to become a college president or to have another child, sees Heinz's dilemma as a choice between selfishness and sacrifice. For Heinz to steal the drug, given the circumstances of his life, which she infers from his inability to pay two thousand dollars, he would have "to do something which is not in his best interest, in that he is going to get sent away, and that is a supreme sacrifice, a sacrifice which I would say a person truly in love might be willing to make." However, not to steal the drug "would be selfish on his part. He would have to feel guilty about not allowing her a chance to live longer." Heinz's decision to steal is considered not in terms of the logical priority of life over property, which justifies its rightness, but rather in terms of the actual consequences that stealing would have for a man of limited means and little social power.

Considered in the light of its probable outcomes—his wife dead, or Heinz in jail, brutalized by the violence of that experience and his life compromised by a record of felony—the dilemma itself changes. Its resolution has less to do with the relative weights of life and property in an abstract moral conception than with the collision between two lives, formerly conjoined but now in opposition, where the continuation of one life can occur only at the expense of the other. This construction makes clear why judgment revolves around the issue of sacrifice and why guilt becomes the inevitable concomitant of either resolution.

Demonstrating the reticence noted in women's moral judgments, Ruth explains her reluctance to judge in terms of her belief:

> I think that everybody's existence is so different that I kind of
> say to myself, "That might be something that I wouldn't do,"
> but I can't say that it is right or wrong for that person. I can
> only deal with what is appropriate for me to do when I am
> faced with specific problems.

Asked if she would apply to others her own injunction against hurting, she replies:

> I can't say that it is wrong. I can't say that it is right or that
> it's wrong, because I don't know what the person did that the
> other person did something to hurt him. So it is not right that
> the person got hurt, but it is right that the person who just lost
> the job has got the anger up and out. It doesn't put any bread
> on his table, but it is released. I don't mean to be copping out.
> I really am trying to see how to answer these questions for
> you.

Her difficulty in arriving at definitive answers to moral questions,
her sense of strain with the construction of Heinz's problem, stems
from the divergence between these questions and her own frame of
reference:

> I don't even think I use the words *right* and *wrong* anymore,
> and I know I don't use the word *moral,* because I am not sure
> I know what it means. We are talking about an unjust society,
> we are talking about a whole lot of things that are not right,
> that are truly wrong—to use the word that I don't use very
> often—and I have no control to change that. If I could change
> it, I certainly would, but I can only make my small contribu-
> tion from day to day, and if I don't intentionally hurt some-
> body, that is my contribution to a better society. And so a
> chunk of that contribution is also not to pass judgment on
> other people, particularly when I don't know the circum-
> stances of why they are doing certain things.

The reluctance to judge remains a reluctance to hurt, but one
that stems not from a sense of personal vulnerability but rather
from a recognition of the limitation of judgment itself. The deference of the conventional feminine perspective thus continues at the
postconventional level, not as moral relativism but rather as part of

a reconstructed moral understanding. Moral judgment is renounced in an awareness of the psychological and social determination of human behavior, at the same time that moral concern is reaffirmed in recognition of the reality of human pain and suffering:

> I have a real thing about hurting people and always have, and that gets a little complicated at times, because, for example, you don't want to hurt your child. I don't want to hurt my child, but if I don't hurt her sometimes, then that's hurting her more, you see, so that was a terrible dilemma for me.

Moral dilemmas are terrible in that they entail hurt. Ruth sees Heinz's decision as "the result of anguish: Who am I hurting? Why do I have to hurt them?" The morality of Heinz's theft is not in question, given the circumstances that necessitated it. What is at issue is his willingness to substitute himself for his wife and become, in her stead, the victim of exploitation by a society which breeds and legitimizes the druggist's irresponsibility and whose injustice is thus manifest in the very occurrence of the dilemma.

The same sense that the wrong questions are being asked is evident in the response of another woman who justifies Heinz's action on a similar basis, saying, "I don't think that exploitation should really be a right." When women begin to make direct moral statements, the issues they repeatedly address are those of exploitation and hurt. In doing so, they raise the issue of nonviolence in precisely the same psychological context that brings Erikson (1969) to pause in his consideration of the truth of Gandhi's life. In the pivotal letter that he addresses to Gandhi and around which the judgment of his book turns, Erikson confronts the contradiction between the philosophy of nonviolence that informed Gandhi's dealing with the British and the psychological violence that marred his relationships with his family and with the children of the ashram. It was this contradiction, Erikson confesses, "which almost brought *me* to the point where I felt unable to continue writing *this* book because I seemed to sense the presence of a kind of untruth in the very protestation of truth; of something unclean when all the words spelled out an unreal purity; and, above all, of displaced violence where nonviolence was the professed issue" (pp. 230–231).

In an effort to untangle the relationship between the spiritual truth of Satyagraha and the truth of his own psychoanalytic understanding, Erikson reminds Gandhi that, "Truth, you once said, 'excludes the use of violence because man is not capable of knowing the absolute truth and therefore is not competent to punish' " (p. 241). The affinity between Satyagraha and psychoanalysis lies in their shared commitment to seeing life as an "experiment in truth," in their being "somehow joined in a universal 'therapeutics,' committed to the Hippocratic principle that one can test truth (or the healing power inherent in a sick situation) only by action which avoids harm—or better, by action which maximizes mutuality and minimizes the violence caused by unilateral coercion or threat" (p. 247). Thus Erikson takes Gandhi to task for his failure to acknowledge the relativity of truth. This failure is manifest in the coercion of his claim to exclusive possession of the truth, his "unwillingness to learn from *anybody anything* except what was approved by the 'inner voice' " (p. 236). This claim led Gandhi, in the guise of love, to impose his truth on others without awareness of or regard for the extent to which he thereby did violence to their integrity.

The moral dilemma, arising inevitably out of a conflict of truths, is by definition a "sick situation" in that its either/or formulation leaves no room for an outcome that does not do violence. The resolution of such dilemmas, however, lies not in the self-deception of rationalized violence: "I was" said Gandhi, "a cruelly kind husband. I regarded myself as her teacher and so harassed her out of my blind love for her" (p. 233). The resolution lies rather in the replacement of the underlying antagonism with a mutuality of respect and care.

Gandhi, whom Kohlberg cites as exemplifying the sixth stage of moral judgment and whom Erikson initially sought as a model of an adult ethical sensibility, is criticized by a judgment that refuses to look away from or condone the infliction of harm. In denying the validity of his wife's reluctance to open her home to strangers and in blinding himself to the different reality of adolescent sexuality and temptation, Gandhi compromised in his everyday life the ethic of nonviolence to which, in principle and in public, he steadfastly adhered.

The blind willingness to sacrifice people to truth, however, has always been the danger of an ethics abstacted from life. This willingness links Gandhi to the biblical Abraham, who prepared to sacrifice the life of his son in order to demonstrate the integrity and supremacy of his faith. Both men, in the limitations of their fatherhood, stand in implicit contrast to the woman who comes before Solomon and verifies her motherhood by relinquishing truth in order to save the life of her child. It is the ethics of an adulthood that has become principled at the expense of care that Erikson comes to criticize in his assessment of Gandhi's life.

This same criticism is dramatized explicitly as a contrast between the sexes in *The Merchant of Venice*, where Shakespeare goes through an extraordinary complication of sexual identity, dressing a male actor as a female character who in turn poses as a male judge, in order to bring into the masculine citadel of justice the feminine plea for mercy. The limitation of the contractual conception of justice is illustrated through the absurdity of its literal execution, while the need to "make exceptions all the time" is demonstrated contrapuntally in the matter of the rings. Portia, in calling for mercy, argues for that resolution in which no one is hurt, and as the men are forgiven for their failure to keep both their rings and their word, Antonio in turn forgoes his "right" to ruin Shylock.

The abortion study suggests that women impose a distinctive construction on moral problems, seeing moral dilemmas in terms of conflicting responsibilities. This construction was traced through a sequence of three perspectives, each perspective representing a more complex understanding of the relationship between self and other and each transition involving a critical reinterpretation of the conflict between selfishness and responsibility. The sequence of women's moral judgment proceeds from an initial concern with survival to a focus on goodness and finally to a reflective understanding of care as the most adequate guide to the resolution of conflicts in human relationships. The abortion study demonstrates the centrality of the concepts of responsibility and care in women's constructions of the moral domain, the close tie in women's thinking between conceptions of the self and of morality, and ultimately the need for an expanded developmental theory that includes, rather than rules out from consideration, the differences in the feminine voice. Such an inclusion seems essential, not only for explaining the development of women but also for understanding in both sexes the characteristics and precursors of an adult moral conception.

4 Crisis and Transition

N THE FILM *Wild Strawberries,* Marianne, the pregnant
daughter-in-law of old Isak Borg, travels with him to Lund,
where he is to receive the highest honor of his medical profession. She is returning to end her marriage, given her husband Evald's position that she must choose between him
and the child. Hoping to avert this decision, she went to his
father for help, impelled by "some idiotic idea" that the old doctor
would heal the division. Instead, she found "well hidden behind
[his] mask of old-fashioned charm and friendliness," the same wall
of "inflexible opinions" that encircled his son's opposition, a lack of
consideration for others and a refusal to "listen to anyone but [him-
self]." Just as Evald claimed to have made absolutely clear his wish
not to have a child, explaining that he had no "need (for) a responsibility which will force me to exist another day longer than I want
to," so his father wanted no part in Marianne's marital problems,
saying that he did not "give a damn about them" and had "no respect for suffering of the soul." Yet when in the car, Borg offers the
opinion that he and Evald are "very much alike. We have our principles ... and I know Evald understands and respects me," he is
startled when Marianne replies, "That may be true, but he also
hates you."

With this counterpoint between the old man's principled with-
drawal and the young woman's efforts to sustain connection, the action of the film begins. The link established between Borg's "evil
and frightening dreams" and Marianne's realization that "it would

be terrible to have to depend on you in any way" ties the despair of his old age to the ongoing failure of family relationships. Erikson (1976), taking Bergman's film as his text for explicating the cycle of life, cites Marianne as the catalyst who precipitates the crisis that leads to change. He compares Marianne to Cordelia in driving to the surface an old man's despair, confronting him with the source of his discomfort by revealing the disturbing but liberating truths of relationships. And Erikson shows how this confrontation spurs the sequence of memories and dreams through which Borg retraces his steps through the stages of life, arriving at intimacy, the point where he failed. He dreams of an examination in which he forgets that "a doctor's first duty is to ask forgiveness," and he cannot tell if a woman is dead or alive. The examiner pronounces him "guilty of guilt." The sentence: "loneliness, of course." Thus connecting the present with the past, Borg comes to acknowledge his own defeat ("that I am dead, although I live") but in doing so, he releases the future, turning to offer Marianne his help.

Erikson, defining Marianne's role in breaking the cycle of repetition that had extended across generations a cold loneliness "more frightening than death itself," identifies the "dominant determination to care" in this "quiet, independent girl with her naked, observant eyes." Yet in tracing the development of the virtue of care, which he views as the strength of adult life, he turns repeatedly to the lives of men. Since in life-cycle theory, as in the film, Marianne's story remains untold, it is never clear how she came to see what she sees or to know what she knows.

In the abortion decision study, women described dilemmas similar to that which Marianne faced, and an analysis of their descriptions reveals a sequence in the understanding of responsibility and relationships. This sequence, derived by comparing different perspectives on the abortion choice, was logically constructed by considering the conflicts between these perspectives manifest in women's thought. But while distinctions can be drawn through a comparative analysis and a progression charted by following the logic of thought, only through time can development be traced. Thus, by looking directly at women's lives over time, it becomes possible to test, in a preliminary way, whether the changes predicted by theory fit the reality of what in fact takes place. In comparing interviews conducted at the time of the abortion decision with those that occurred at the end of the following year, I use the magnification of crisis to reveal the process of developmental transition and to delineate the pattern of change. In doing so, I draw on the work of Piaget (1968) in identifying conflict as the harbinger of growth and also on the work of Erikson (1964) who, in charting development through crisis, demonstrates how a heightened vulnerability signals the emergence of a potential strength, creating a dangerous opportunity for growth, "a turning point for better or worse" (p. 139).

Twenty-three women were contacted for the follow-up study, and twenty-one agreed to take part. The interview was similar in format to the one conducted at the time of choice. Although the discussion of the abortion decision was retrospective, the questions asked were essentially the same, about the choice and about the woman's view of her life and herself. On a life-outcome scale constructed to measure the occurrence and direction of change over the year and based on the women's descriptions of their relationships and work and of their feelings about their lives, eight of the women's lives had improved, nine had stayed the same, and four had changed for the worse (Belenky, 1978; Gilligan and Belenky, 1980).

The women considered in this analysis are those for whom the pregnancy precipitated a crisis and led to an encounter with defeat. The sorrow of this encounter and the loss experienced in the process of change highlight the importance of the crisis itself and reveal the predicament of human relationships. As pregnancy signifies a connection of the greatest magnitude in terms of responsibility, so abortion poses a dilemma in which there is no way of acting without consequences to other and self. In underlining the reality of interdependence and the irrevocability of choice, the abortion dilemma magnifies the issues of responsibility and care that derive from the fact of relationship. Freud, in tracing development through the exposure of crisis, compares the psyche under stress to a crystal that is thrown to the floor and breaks "not into haphazard pieces [but] comes apart along its lines of cleavage into fragments whose boundaries, though they were invisible, were predetermined by the crystal's structure" (1933, p. 59). In extending this metaphor to a consideration of relationships under stress, I call attention to the way that the fracturing of relationships reveals the lines of their articulation, exposing the psychic structuring of connection in the concepts of morality and self.

The studies of women's lives over time portray the role of cri-

sis in transition and underline the possibilities for growth and despair that lie in the recognition of defeat. The studies of Betty and
Sarah elucidate the transitions in the development of an ethic of
care. The shifts in concern from survival to goodness and from
goodness to truth are elaborated through time in these two women's
lives. Both studies illustrate the potential of crisis to break a cycle
of repetition and suggest that crisis itself may signal a return to a
missed opportunity for growth. These portraits of transition are followed by depictions of despair, illustrations of moral nihilism in
women who could find no answer to the question "Why care?"

Betty was sixteen when she went to an abortion clinic for a
second abortion within a period of six months. The counselor, concerned about the repetition, denied her request to have an abortion
that day and referred Betty to the study in order to provide an opportunity for her to reflect on her decision and consider what she
was doing. Although the story of Betty, an adopted adolescent who
had a history of repeated abortions, disorderly conduct, and reform
school, is stark in demonstrating life lived at the extreme, it illuminates the potential for change in a seemingly sparse life. It also depicts the shift in concern from survival to goodness that marks the
transition from "selfishness" to responsibility.

In the first interview, Betty begins by saying that the second
pregnancy, like the first, was not her fault. Feeling both helpless
and powerless to obtain contraception for herself, because she did
not have any money and she believed she needed her parents' permission, she also felt powerless to deal with her boyfriend's continuing harassment. In the end, she gave in to his assurance that he
knew what he was doing and would not get her pregnant, influenced by her belief that if she refused, he would break up with
her. Since she had asked both him and her mother for contraception without success, Betty explains that she became pregnant because no one was willing to help. Wishing now that she had used
contraception, but seeing others as responsible for the fact that she
did not, she says that when she first found out about the pregnancy,
she did not know what to do:

> I wanted to kill myself, because I just couldn't face the fact. I
> knew that I wanted to get an abortion. I knew that I couldn't
> have the kid, but I just couldn't face the fact of going through
> that again.

Her reference is to the physical pain that she experienced the previous time.

Her reluctance to break up with her boyfriend stemmed from the fact that he treated her differently from anyone she ever knew: "He did everything for me. (*What kinds of things?*) Called me, picked me up, take me anywhere I wanted to go, buy me cigarettes, buy me beer if I wanted." Given her expectation that if she went to bed with him, he would continue to meet her needs, her disappointment was great when she discovered that, "after I went to bed with him, he just wanted me to do everything that he wanted to do. I was more like a wife than a girlfriend, and I didn't like that." Describing the relationship as one of exchange, she concludes that he "was really one-way," seeking only to meet his needs and disregarding "the fact that I wanted more freedom." Angry as well at the counselor who interfered with her wish to have an abortion, she nevertheless feels that the counselor "just wanted to make sure that my mind would be stable when I left there. I think it's good, because at least they care."

Perhaps in part because of this demonstration of care, Betty begins to reflect on the way that she has taken care of herself. Saying that perhaps the pregnancy is her fault, she attributes it to her failure to listen to herself. She listened to others because she believed that she would "get something out of it, or it will make things better and they will stop bothering me." But since these reasons have been belied by her experience, she begins to reflect on the assumptions that previously guided her behavior and her thought. Her consideration of the abortion only in terms of physical pain, her wish to keep the pregnancy secret in order to avoid getting a "wicked reputation," her concern about maintaining her freedom rather than having to do things for others, all indicate her preoccupation with her own needs and her struggle to ensure her own survival in a world perceived as exploitative and threatening, a world in which she experiences herself as uncared for and alone. This construction of social reality is vividly apparent in her justification for Heinz's stealing the drug:

> The druggist is ripping him off and his wife is dying, so the druggist deserves to be ripped off. (*Is it the right thing to do?*) Probably. I think survival is one of the first things in life that people fight for. I think it is the most important thing, more important than stealing. Stealing might be wrong, but if you

have to steal to survive yourself, or even kill, that is what you should do. (*Why is that?*) Preservation of oneself, I think, is the most important thing. It comes before anything in life. A lot of people say sex is the most important thing to a lot of people, but I think that preservation of oneself is the most important thing to people.

Betty's overriding concern with survival in her description of human relationships reflects her experience of being an adopted child and thus one whose survival seems particularly endangered. Betty's feelings about her own precarious survival come to light as she shifts her focus in the abortion decision from her own needs to those of the child. This shift is marked by the appearance of moral language when she says that "abortion is *the right thing to do* in a situation like mine, if someone is in the middle of school or if they have to go back to school like I do." The consideration of her own needs from the somewhat different perspective of a perceived obligation to her parents to go back to school leads then to an extension of moral concern from herself to the child: "It would be unfair of me to have a baby, unfair to the baby more than to me."

At the time of the previous pregnancy, which occurred when she was raped while hitchhiking, she "just couldn't stand the thought of the baby," but this time, she has "thought about it a lot." Her use of the concept of fairness indicates the moral nature of her concern, which emerges from her recognition of the connection between the baby and herself:

> Thinking about the baby makes me feel kind of strange, because I am adopted, and I was thinking, like my mother didn't want me, otherwise she wouldn't have put me up for adoption. But I was thinking if I could have been an abortion or maybe was intended to be, or something, and that kind of gives me strange feelings about it.

Connecting present with past in tying her feelings about the baby to her own feelings of having been in some sense an unwanted child, Betty begins to think about her own biological mother's feelings for her, hoping that maybe she was wanted in the sense that her mother "really loved the guy but couldn't take care of me."

But in shifting her perspective across generations, Betty also thinks of the future and envisions herself as capable of becoming a mother who could take care of a child. Through the notion of fairness, she articulates her wish to give to her own child what she wanted to have: "I don't think it would be fair to give life to a child if it couldn't have its own mother." In thinking about the baby, she also comes to think about herself in a new way, to realize through the connection of the pregnancy that caring for the baby means taking care of herself:

> In a lot of ways this pregnancy has helped me because I have stopped getting high and stopped drinking, and this is the first time in three years I stopped. And now that I have, I know that I can do it, and I am just going to completely stop. (*How did the pregnancy help you to do that?*) Because when I first got pregnant, I wasn't sure what I was going to do, and when I first found out, I thought to myself, "This time it was my fault, and I have to keep the baby." But then, I stopped drinking and stopped getting high because I didn't want to hurt the baby. And then, after a couple of weeks, I thought about it again, and I said, "No, I can't have it, because I have to go back to school."

Just as Betty begins to take care of herself out of her wish not to hurt the baby, so her sense of having to go back to school stems in part from "the thought about having a kid and not having an education and not having any skills." Recognizing that she is unable to take care of a child without any means of support and believing that the baby might already be hurt by the drugs she took before the pregnancy was confirmed, Betty sees the need to take care of herself before she will be able to care for a child: "I guess I am going to start having to take care of myself better. Sooner or later you have to make up your mind to start taking care of yourself, being your own person instead of having everybody else tell you what to do."

In the follow-up interview one year later, the language of egocentric concern has disappeared, and the language of relationship and care that was evident initially in Betty's talk about herself and the child now extends to describe her life. The shift from concern with survival to concern with goodness, which marks the transition from selfishness to responsibility in her thought, is paralleled by the changes that have occurred in Betty's life over the intervening year.

Recalling the time following the abortion, she describes a period of depression and recounts her feelings of sadness and loss as she tells of giving up a puppy, staying at home all day watching television, fighting with her mother, and gaining weight: "I was the heaviest I have ever been, and I was so depressed. I just stayed home all winter. I would never go out of the house, I would be so ashamed." But then a change occurred in June:

> I said I have to lose, and it was such a change for me, because I had been fat for so many years. And being thin, I never knew what it was like to be able to wear clothes that looked good. I just felt dynamite, because so many people and so many guys were trying to go out with me. It was the first summer I was able to wear a bathing suit.

This dramatic change began at the time that the baby would have been born, had the pregnancy continued. In the lives of other women as well this proved to be a significant date, marking the denouement of the crisis and signaling the turn for better or worse. Among the women for whom the abortion decision signified the beginning of a developmental advance—a new assumption of responsibility, a confrontation with truth—this tended to be the time when depression ended, as though the duration of the pregnancy marked a natural period of mourning whose completion led to activities that resulted in substantial improvements in a woman's life. For the women whose choice signified, in their own terms, a retreat, this was the time when things fell apart.

For Betty, the improvement is marked. After years of trouble at home, in school, and in the community, she is enrolled at the time of the second interview in an alternative school, engaged in her work and actively participating in the school's community life. She has a steady relationship with a boyfriend, which sounds substantially different from relationships she previously described in that activities of mutual care and affection have replaced coercive and exploitative deals. Betty is also preparing, with the encouragement of her school, to enter a community college the following fall.

The change in Betty's moral understanding is evident in her response to Heinz's dilemma. She now says that Heinz should steal the drug "because his wife is dying, near death, and he loves his wife." Although she explains that she is going to "answer the same as before," referring to the choice itself, the structure of her justification has fundamentally changed. Whereas previously she indicated the primacy of survival, now she emphasizes the importance of relationship. Where she spoke of entitlement, now she speaks of guilt. Heinz should steal "because he loves his wife, and if she dies, he is going to feel like he could have done something but he didn't." Thus security, which she formerly saw as self-protection in an exploitative world where everyone gets ripped off, now depends on relationships with others, on the expression of love and care.

The transformation of Betty's moral judgments corresponds to the change in her view of herself. In the first interview she described herself as "kind of hard to get along with," willful, impulsive, and "easily led"; in the second, she says, "I think I am a person who likes challenge. I like to learn. I like things that are interesting. I like to talk to people. I am very sensitive." Asked whether she thinks there has been a change in the way she sees herself, she says: "Definitely. Now I really care about myself, and then I didn't really care. I was so disgusted with everything. Now I am starting to get a better attitude, and I feel like I can change a lot of things that I thought before I would never be able to change." No longer feeling so powerless, exploited, alone, and endangered, Betty feels more in control. Things have "changed drastically" over a year in a way that convinces her she can "make it in life."

Just as the world of morality has replaced a world in which everyone was getting ripped off, so too the world of mutuality has succeeded relationships that were disappointingly "one way." Although Betty remembers the time of the pregnancy as a hard time, she thinks it may be "better to learn the hard way, because then it stays. You really learn. It sticks with you. It just stays with you."

Thus in Betty's life, the second pregnancy brought to the surface conflicts from her past and exposed contradictions in the present. The intervention of the abortion counselor, who cared enough to interfere with the emerging pattern of abortions and to provide Betty with an opportunity for thought and reflection, initiated a clinical crisis and precipitated a developmental transition. The process of growth, which consumed most of the year that separated the first and second interviews, was marked by a period of mourning, disorganization, and despair.

At the end of the year, in the second interview, Betty demonstrates a new understanding of the events of her past and a new way of thinking about the future. Past conflicts have been revisited in a way that allows her to address the present issues of her adolescent development and to articulate a clear sense of herself as a responsible person, in her relationships with her family, her boyfriend, and in her school community. Although the second pregnancy recapitulates the past and illustrates the repetitive phenomenon of acting out, it also looks forward to the future, confronting Betty with the issues of responsibility and care that were critical to her development.

Robert Coles (1964) observes that crisis can lead to growth when it presents an opportunity to confront impediments to further development. To illustrate this point, he describes John Washington, a black adolescent living in poverty, whose parents showed symptoms of "serious mental disorder." Yet in volunteering to participate in the desegregation of the Atlanta schools, John began a progress toward growth under conditions of extraordinary stress. When Coles asked him what enabled him to do it, John said: "That school glued me together; it made me stronger than I ever thought I could be, and so now I don't think I'll be able to forget what happened. I'll probably be different for the rest of my life" (p. 122).

The notion that development occurs through an encounter with stress, that conflict provides an opportunity for growth, is at the center of Coles' analysis. Under different circumstances of stress, Betty makes a similar point. Comparing her present with her past, she says:

> I am really happy with where my life is going now. Compared with last year, it has changed so much and is so much better. I feel better about what I am doing. I get up in the morning and I go to school. I was just sitting around for a year-and-a-half doing nothing. I wasn't going anywhere in life. I didn't know what I was doing, and now I feel I have a direction in a way, I know what I am interested in.

Following the denouement of the crisis, Betty is anchored firmly in life, seeing herself as a person with a direction, responsible in caring for others and for herself.

Josie, the seventeen-year-old whose thinking illustrated the transition from selfishness to responsibility, reports similar changes in her life after the abortion choice. By the second interview she also has "changed a lot, because I was doing a lot of drugs and everything and I had a lot of problems with my parents and with the court and stuff. It is sort of like a stage I was going through, and I look back on it and I don't see how I could have done it. It is like I grew out of it. I still have problems sometimes, but not like I used to, and I don't do drugs anymore." She also is back in school, collaborating with a teacher on a book about adolescence. But her retrospective description of her abortion decision foreshadows the problems of the second perspective. In the first interview, she claimed the abortion decision and described it as the "responsible" as opposed to the "selfish" choice, as a move toward becoming "more mature in ways of making decisions realistically and taking care of myself." In the second interview she says that she was "pressured into it" and that she "didn't have any choice " Reporting, like Betty, a period of depression following the abortion and preceding the dramatic improvement in her life, she is caught between her own perception that the abortion was a responsible decision and the conventional interpretation of abortion as a selfish choice.

She says that she is against abortion but then criticizes that statement as "hypocritical" and criticizes as well the people who "say it is murder but have never been in the position of being pregnant and not having anyone to help them out and not having any money." Explaining that if she had had the child, she would have "ended up on welfare for the next six years and my kid has no father," she then does not "know if that makes sense." Similarly, she does not know who made the decision. "I think a year ago, I might have been saying that it was my own decision and stuff, and in a way I think that it was my own decision, but I don't know." Seeing herself now as good and responsible, Josie does not want to be selfish and bad. Like Betty, who says in the second interview that "thinking about abortion, I don't know what to think, what it is," Josie does not know whether the abortion was a selfish or a responsible choice. As the insight of the transition yields to the dichotomy of the second position, Josie cannot decide whether abortion is "morally wrong" or whether it "makes sense."

Sarah, a woman of twenty-five, lively and engaging at the time of the first interview, is intelligent, humorous, and sad as she describes her experience of self-defeat. Pregnant again by the same man and confronting a second abortion, she sees the hopelessness of the relationship. Since she discovered the first pregnancy at a time when he had left her, she found the abortion "almost a pleasant experience, like expelling that man from my life." This time, however, "the reality that this is a baby just sort of dumped me out on my head." The crisis she faces was precipitated by her lover's statement that he would leave her unless she aborted the child.

Seeing no way to raise a child by herself in the absence of emotional and financial support, Sarah confronts the reality of her situation and begins to reflect on her life. She is caught by the contradiction between her view of herself as responsible and good and her belief that it is "irresponsible" and "selfish" to have a second abortion. However, her thinking is complicated by the fact that what seems the "responsible thing to do," namely paying for one's mistakes by having the child, suddenly appears also to be "selfish," —bringing a child into the world "to assuage my guilt." Given these apparent contradictions, she is unable to find the good or self-sacrificing solution, since either way she can construe her actions as serving not only others but also herself.

But in facing the choice precipitated by her lover's exclusion of the child, Sarah notices her own exclusion of herself. Noting that her self-sacrifice sustained a relationship which could not sustain a child, she shifts her perception of the situation and sees the pregnancy not only as a defeat but also as a confrontation with truth:

> It is a stress situation that brings out all the things in my relationship with [the father] that I had just been grinding along with all this time and just could have ground along with indefinitely. And now, wow, there it is, panorama, you cannot hide from it anymore. And so you might say that it becomes a very auspicious time. I am sorry.

Because the pregnancy reveals the unviability of the relationship, Sarah sees it as auspicious, an augury of change; but since it also reveals a viable child, it is an occasion of regret. To Sarah, taking responsibility for ending this life means taking responsibility for herself as well, bringing herself into the compass of her moral concern and facing the truth of her relationships. In doing so, she calls into question her former view of herself as a good victim of circumstance, acting responsibly while suffering from the consequences of others' irresponsible behavior. This view is countered by the realization that she has more power than she thought and in fact "knew exactly what was happening."

For Sarah, confronting the limits of her pattern of disappointing relationships means not only dealing with the residues of her past, namely her parents' divorce and her image of her mother as endlessly self-sacrificing and inducing guilt, but also confronting in the present the question of judgment, by whose standards will she guide and measure her life. Maintaining that she is "tired of always bowing to other people's standards," she draws on the Quaker tradition she has joined in asserting that "nobody can force anything on you because your first duty is to your inner voice that speaks what is right." Yet when the inner voice replaces outer ones as the arbiter of morality and truth, it frees her from the coercion of others, but leaves her with the responsibility for judgment and choice.

The ultimate choice is abortion: "How can you take responsibility for taking a life?" but also how can you bring a child into the world in order to "assuage your guilt?" The "turning point" for Sarah comes in the realization that in this situation there is no way of acting that avoids hurt to others as well as to herself, and in this sense, no choice that is "right." Seeing no resolution that does not leave conflict, no way of acting that does not exclude, she finds in the constraint of this dilemma the limits of her previous mode of thought. Thus Sarah reconsiders the opposition between selfishness and responsibility, realizing that this opposition fails to represent the truth of the connection between the child and herself. Concluding that there is no formula for whom to exclude and seeing the necessity of including herself, she decides that in her present situation, abortion is the better choice, while realizing that, if the situation were different, the choice would go the other way.

Although Sarah is able in this crisis to envision herself and her life in a new way, the realization of this vision follows a difficult course. Because of her wish to marry and have a child, she is attached to this pregnancy; as a result, its ending signifies a great loss. The process of mourning is vividly described by Sarah, who called at the end of six months to say that, since she was leaving the city, perhaps I would like to interview her then. As a result, for Sarah the second interview takes place toward the end of the time through which the pregnancy would have extended, had it gone to term—during the period reported by other women to be a time of disorganization and distress.

When Sarah arrived for the second interview, she was almost unrecognizable, looking gaunt, frightened, and subdued, with little of her former liveliness in evidence. It had been, she says, a difficult time and one of considerable loss. Following the abortion, she had a series of illnesses, which she attributes to the strain of "the whole upheaval" of ending the relationship with her boyfriend, leaving her job, and making several moves. Yet through her distress she continues to focus on the issue of truth, unraveling the events that led to the crisis and in the end confronting herself:

> I think it was very nearly a conscious decision to get pregnant. I was thinking about kids a lot, having a dream or two occasionally. It was something I really wanted to do. When I was having intercourse, it would run across my mind, "Gee, it would be nice to get pregnant"—the whole thing. So it was definitely accidently on purpose. It was not even that far removed. It was almost exactly on purpose.

Realizing that her purpose was to force the issue of commitment in a relationship where she already knew what the outcome would be, she also realizes that she was masking the truth and "deluding" herself:

> The pregnancy really forced all this out into the open. Whereas if I hadn't gotten pregnant, I might have been able to go to another solution, because everything that was wrong about the relationship was so clear that even I could not fool myself anymore. And I had done a pretty good job of it for a couple of years. So the pregnancy served its purpose. And yet, on the other hand, I really did want to get pregnant, not just to serve the purpose of either getting me further into or completely out of the relationship, but I really did want to have a child, and I still do.

As a result, "now I just feel a lot of loss."

In the first interview, she described herself as "tired" and "frustrated" by trying indirectly to get other people to respond to her needs by being "hard working," "patient," virtuous in a way that led only to defeat: "It's got to stop. It can't go on forever, and I've repeated the same mistakes several times now, and I think that's enough." In the second interview, the self Sarah described has finally fallen apart:

> (*How would you describe yourself to yourself?*) I don't know. I would say I am gathering up the last. I just feel that everything has been blasted away, and after the last blast I am

making a desperate leap to get back up. Although I am feeling a lot better now than I have for a long time, physically anyway, since I decided [to leave the city]. It occurred to me when I started packing that it was kind of ironic. You think the important thing when you are leaving to go somewhere is that you are taking your body somewhere else and of course your belongings follow along, but it seems almost as if my belongings outweigh me because that is all there is left of me. I just feel really beaten down, lost, and I feel really tired. There seemed to be more substance to the actual material possessions that I was putting in the trunk than there was to me. I thought, "There is more to the trash you fill your life with than there is to you."

Thus Sarah conveys her sense of having in some way disappeared, leaving fragments that do not cohere, a body and a trunk filled with possessions, the remnants of her former self. Looking back on the abortion, she finds that it too has outstripped her understanding, that she can no longer find a way to encompass the thoughts and the feelings which it evoked:

Because being a woman and being pregnant, there is something you can't deny, that you can't explain away. There are all the good reasons in the world. I am sure I did the right thing. It would have been hell for that poor kid and for me too. But I don't know if you can get what I am getting at, because I can't get what I am getting at. The reasons just don't fill up the whole. It's just that somehow the whole is larger than the sum of its parts when you take it apart. There is just something that happens when you put it all together that is not there when you take it apart and try to put it together, and I don't know what that is.

In trying to find the wholeness of an event which has dissolved into parts, Sarah illuminates the moment of transition, between the old way and the new. No longer able to fit her experience into her understanding, not "knowing what it is" that has led to such desolation, she has reached the point in crisis where all that she feels is the loss. A sense of loss and mourning pervades the second interview. It appears in her comment that, as she thinks of leaving the city, "it just sort of grips me that I am leaving a baby here." It emerges in her feeling "that I had misplaced something, and then I realized, 'You have left your baby across town,' " and also in her belief that, "if someday I have three children, I will also feel I have three children and two others that are not with us right now. I have five, and here are three of them."

To Sarah, the importance of remembering lies in not repeating the past, since she attributes the second abortion to the fact that she never dealt with the first. Feeling "really sad" and "not in control anymore," she "set the ball rolling, and now I am sort of riding. This whole summer has been really, really crazy," a period of "great personal upheaval," a time of disorganization, mourning, crisis, and grief—and yet also, in her eyes, a time of change.

Returning to the city a year after the abortion, Sarah came to talk for a third time, speaking of change and describing it as "a visual thing—like coming around full circle, like where I started out on this whole journey." The journey began around the age of twelve, when she started to see herself as a separate person in her family:

> My childhood was just that. It was just a childhood. And then, I remembered making a conscious decision, somewhere around twelve years old. All of a sudden I see myself as being a separate person in the unit of my family, and all of a sudden I'm becoming very aware of things that I like, things that I think are all right and that nobody else in my family thinks are all right, and I'm not going to turn out the way my mother thinks I am, based on a whole life in which the outcome is just expectations which she has voiced for me. So what I had to do was keep the peace until I could get out of there, just sort of toeing the line, just barely toeing the line, and that's what I did.

The upheaval in her family that followed her parents' divorce complicated Sarah's development at that time and left a legacy of issues that entwined with the themes of adolescence, raising questions of identity and morality which she then set out on her own to resolve. Having "tried a lot of different ways of living," she sought to discover what was of value in life:

> I wanted just literally to throw away all the moral values that I'd been taught and decide for myself which ones were important to me. And I figured that I'd know which ones were important if I missed it, if I pitched it out the window and said,

"To hell with that," and then came up a few months later really feeling the pinch because that wasn't there in my life. Then I'd know *that* was important. So just throwing everything out and then just picking selectively what I wanted. And I've sort of surprised myself because I've come back around, not to the way of life that my mother would have had me live, but a lot more like it than I thought. And it's so interesting when I look back and I think, "Hmm, I never thought I'd turn out that way."

Reiterating with more confidence and clarity her discovery of an inner voice, she says that her decisions previously "were based elsewhere, I'm not really sure where, but it was coming from somewhere else." In contrast, now she feels "really connected with my insides, really good. I just feel strong in a way I'm not aware of having felt, really in control of my life, not just sort of randomly drifting along." As Sarah describes her feeling of being in control, her pronouns shift from *it* to *I*, marking the end of the time of just drifting along. Sarah had criticized the opposition of selfishness and responsibility at the time of the first interview. Realizing the truth of her own participation in the events that led to her defeat and the indirection of her search for response, she saw the abortion decision as a choice to include herself, not to rule herself out from consideration but to consider her own needs as well as those of others in deciding what was the best thing to do.

But the integration of this insight into Sarah's life, the completion of the transition precipitated by the crisis, entailed a long and painful process that lasted for most of a year. Through this experience, she became more reflective: "I see the way I am and watch the way I make choices, the things I do." And she is now committed to building her life on a "strong foundation" of "surprisingly old wisdoms" with respect to her work and her relationships. Saying that "you create the crisis yourself so that you have to deal with it," she changes the image of her development from a circle to a spiral, since coming full circle implies "having grown to the same place," whereas in a spiral, "instead of coming around to the same place, you're in the same position but you're up somewhere else. You've progressed, and I feel like that's what happened."

The changes in Sarah's life and in her sense of herself are paralleled by changes in her moral judgment, which shifts from a negative to a positive mode, from "deciding who is going to lose the least and who is going to get hurt the least" to a "compassion" that leads to caring and respect for her own and other people's needs. Previously she equated morality with being "law abiding" while at the same time rejecting the law as "stupid." Now she articulates a basis for judging the law in terms of whether or not it is hurting society and whether or not it "puts a barrier" in the way of compassion and respect. As her judgments change from the conventional mode where "right" is defined by others and responsibility rests with them to the reflective mode which entails taking responsibility for herself, her action shifts from a stance of detachment and rebellion to one of commitment in work and relationships.

Sarah, like Betty, illuminates the potential in crisis for developmental transition and demonstrates how the recognition of defeat can signal the discovery of a new way. But the turning point of crisis also contains the potential for nihilism and despair. Sarah's imagery of development, of progressing through a rising spiral of change so that in the end she comes to see the same things in a different light, contrasts with Anne's imagery of defeat, her sense of "going in circles" and losing "the confidence I had in myself." This imagery appears in the second interview with Anne, the woman who illustrated the impasse of the first transition, and conveys her sense of herself as "getting back to something that I was before rather than thinking of anything new." During the intervening year, she has watched her life fall apart. Witnessing relationships end and dropping out of school, Anne feels she has lost her ability "to make a go of it."

This feeling of despair is echoed by Lisa, a fifteen-year-old who, believing in her boyfriend's love, acceded to his wish "not to murder his child." But after she decided not to abort the child, he left her and thus "ruined my life." Isolated at home taking care of the child, dependent on welfare for support, disowned by her father, and abandoned by her boyfriend, she has become unrecognizable to herself:

> I am not the same person I was a year and a half ago. I was a very happy person then. I am just not myself anymore. I feel I lose all my friends now because I am somebody else. I am not me. I don't like myself, and I don't know if other people would either. I don't like the way I am now. That's why I am so unhappy. Before I had the baby, I was free. I had a lot of friends. I was fun to be with. I was happy. I enjoyed a lot of

things, and I am just different now. I'm lonely. I'm quiet. I am
not like I was anymore. I have changed completely.

Previously she described herself as "friendly," but now she
says she is "confused," because "I don't know what to do with my
boyfriend gone. I'm still in love with him, no matter what he has
done, and that really confuses me, because I don't know why I still
do." Caught in a cycle of despair, finding no way to go back to
school and, without school, no way to support herself and the child,
"just confused about everything because I can't get him out of my
mind," she is unable to see how an act of love can have led to such
desolation and loss.

Sophie Tolstoy (1865/1928), making the connection, arrives at
what seems a logical conclusion:

> I have always been told that a woman must love her husband
> and be honourable and be a good wife and mother. They
> write such things in ABC books, and it is all nonsense. The
> thing to do is *not* to love, to be clever and sly, and to hide all
> one's bad points—as if anyone in the world had no faults!
> And the main thing is *not* to love. See what I have done by
> loving him so deeply! It is painful and humiliating; but he
> thinks it is merely silly ... I am nothing but ... a useless crea-
> ture with morning sickness, and a big belly, two rotten teeth,
> and a bad temper, a battered sense of dignity, and a love
> which nobody wants and which nearly drives me insane.

Moral nihilism is the conclusion as well of women who seek,
in having an abortion, to cut off their feelings and not care. Trans-
lating the language of moral ideology into the vernacular of human
relationships, these women ask themselves, "Why care?" in a world
where the strong end relationships. Pregnant and wanting to live in
an expanding circle of family connection, they encounter in their
husbands or lovers an unyielding refusal and rejection. Construing
their caring as a weakness and identifying the man's position with
strength, they conclude that the strong need not be moral and that
only the weak care about relationships. In this construction abortion becomes, for the woman, a test of her strength.

The story takes a number of forms in the lives of women who
have arrived at this point. Its common theme is their abandonment
by others, their common response is to abandon themselves. The

image of Raskolnikov is evoked by a woman, also a student, who became ill at the time the child would have been born and was living alone in a small room. Labeling the abortion an act of murder but one about which she has no regret, she says in the second interview that "there are many ways to kill, and I have seen things that are less merciful than dying." Her lover had said at the time she was pregnant that she could not "depend on him." She herself considered abortion a "selfish choice." It never was clear who had made the decision, since when she said in the first interview that she would have an abortion, she indicated that "the only thing that could make me change my mind is that something would happen and we would be together."

Thus she considers what happened as "not my fault." Describing the abortion as having "cut me off from something I felt a need for, felt very strongly about," she holds herself responsible for the consequences but not for the choice. That is, she holds herself responsible "for someone having to be sacrificed in my having to make that decision." Yet while recognizing that she is "the one who lives with it" and realizing that her world "has become much smaller," she is "not sure if one pays the price." She prefers "to say I did what I did but that there are many forms of killing. If I don't, then nothing means anything, everything is wishy-washy, nothing is real, and you lose any sense of responsibility." Describing herself as acting on another's commission, it remains unclear why she made the choice. She was, she says, "in the wrong boat, anything else would have been absolutely crazy. How can you bring a child into this terrible world?" Focusing on her "responsibility to others," she forgets to respond to herself.

In another version of nihilism, a married woman, pregnant with her second child, had an abortion because her husband said he would leave her if she did not. Holding him responsible, she carried out his decision by becoming "totally numb" and then reenacted the entire situation, becoming pregnant again and having a second abortion. The second time, however, she initially made a decision to have the child. But when her husband then said that he would in fact stay, she saw how unnecessarily she had previously betrayed herself. This recognition then led her to have a second abortion in order to end the marriage in a way that would allow her to take care of herself and her four-year-old child.

Morality, for these women, centers on care, but in the absence of care from others, they are unable to care for a child or them-

selves. The issue is one of responsibility, and life is seen as dependent on relationships. Criticizing those who emphasize "individual
rights" over "issues of responsibility," one woman defines the dilemma of abortion as entailing feelings and thus resisting the imposition of "a stated hierarchy of beliefs":

> Sometimes those hierarchies are good, as long as you look at
> them by themselves, but they fall apart when you try to im-
> pose them on your decisions. They are not organized somehow
> to deal with real life decisions, and it doesn't allow much
> room for responsibility.

The nihilistic position signifies a retreat from care to a concern
with survival, the ultimate self-protective stance. But in attempting
to survive without care, these women return in the end to the truth
about relationships. The student, speaking of her efforts "to be
much more honest with myself about what I wanted and what I
was capable of and how I felt," notes her discovery of her need for
"attachment to other people." Recognizing herself as "much more
an emotional person than I would acknowledge or make room for
before," she strives to be more "careful" with others and more caring about herself. Thus, rather than excluding others and abandoning feelings and care, she becomes more honest about her relationships and more responsive to herself.

The research findings about women's responses to the abortion
dilemma suggest a sequence in the development of an ethic of care
where changes in the conception of responsibility reflect changes in
the experience and understanding of relationships. These findings
were gathered at a particular moment in history, the sample was
small, and the women were not selected to represent a larger population. These constraints preclude the possibility of generalization
and leave to further research the task of sorting out the different
variables of culture, time, occasion, and gender. Additional longitudinal studies of women's moral judgments are needed in order to
refine and validate the sequence described. Studies of people's
thinking about other real dilemmas are needed to clarify the special
features of the abortion choice.

"Crisis reveals character," says one of the women as she
searches for the problem within herself. That crisis also creates
character is the essence of a developmental approach. The changes
described in women's thinking about responsibility and relation-

ships suggest that the capacity for responsibility and care evolves through a coherent sequence of feelings and thoughts. As the events of women's lives and of history intersect with their feelings and thought, a concern with individual survival comes to be branded as "selfish" and to be counterposed to the "responsibility" of a life lived in relationships. And in turn, responsibility becomes, in its conventional interpretation, confused with a responsiveness to others that impedes a recognition of self. The truths of relationship, however, return in the rediscovery of connection, in the realization that self and other are interdependent and that life, however valuable in itself, can only be sustained by care in relationships.

5 Women's Rights and Women's Judgment

W HEN IN THE SUMMER of 1848 Elizabeth Cady Stanton and Lucretia Mott convened a conference at Seneca Falls, New York, to consider "the social, civil and religious condition and rights of women," they presented for adoption a Declaration of Sentiments, modeled on the Declaration of Independence. The issue was simple, and the analogy made their point clear: women are entitled to the rights deemed natural and inalienable by men. The Seneca Falls Conference was spurred by the exclusion of Stanton and Mott, along with other female delegates, from participation in the World Anti-Slavery Convention held in London in 1840. Outraged by their relegation to the balconies to observe the proceedings in which they had come to take part, these women claimed for themselves in 1848 only what they had attempted eight years previously to claim for others, the rights of citizenship in a professedly democratic state. Anchoring this claim in the premise of equality and drawing on the notions of social contract and natural rights, the Seneca Falls Declaration argues no special consideration for women but simply holds "these truths to be self-evident: that all men and women are created equal; that they are endowed by their Creator with certain inalienable rights; that among these are life, liberty, and the pursuit of happiness."

But the claim to rights on the part of women had from the beginning brought them into a seeming opposition with virtue, an opposition challenged by Mary Wollstonecraft in 1792. In "A Vindication of the Rights of Women," she argues that liberty, rather than leading to license, is "the mother of virtue," since enslavement causes not only abjectness and despair but also guile and deceit. Wollstonecraft's "arrogance" in daring "to exert my own reason" and challenge "the mistaken notions that enslave my sex" was subsequently matched by Stanton's boldness in telling a reporter to "put it down in capital letters: SELF-DEVELOPMENT IS A HIGHER DUTY THAN SELF-SACRIFICE. The thing which most retards and militates against women's self-development is self-sacrifice." Countering the accusation of selfishness, the cardinal sin in the ladder of feminine virtue that reached toward an ideal of perfect devotion and self-abnegation, in relation not only to God but to men, these early proponents of women's rights equated self-sacrifice with slavery and asserted that the development of women, like that of men, would serve to promote the general good.

As in claiming rights women claimed responsibility for themselves, so in exercising their reason they began to address issues of responsibility in social relationships. This exercise of reason and the attempt of women to exert control over conditions affecting their lives led, in the latter half of the nineteenth century, to various movements for social reform, ranging from the social purity movements for temperance and public health to the more radical movements for free love and birth control. All of these movements joined in support of suffrage, as women, claiming their intelligence and, to varying degrees, their sexuality as part of their human nature, sought through the vote to include their voices in the shaping of history and to change prevailing practices that were damaging to present and future generations. While the disappointment of suffrage is recorded in the failure of many women to vote and the tendency of others in voting only to second their husbands' opinions, the twentieth century has in fact witnessed the legitimation of many of the rights the early feminists sought.

Given these changes in women's rights, the question arises as to their effect, a question pointed at present both by the renewed struggle for women's rights and by the centennial celebrations of many of the women's colleges to which the feminists' call for women's education gave rise. In tying women's self-development to the exercise of their own reason, the early feminists saw education as critical for women if they were to live under their own control. But as the debate over the current Equal Rights Amendment repeats many of those that occurred in the past, so the issue of women's self-development continues to raise the specter of selfishness, the fear that freedom for women will lead to an abandonment of responsibility in relationships. Thus the dialogue between rights and responsibilities, in its public debate and its psychic representation, focuses the conflicts raised by the inclusion of women in thinking about responsibility and relationships. While this dialogue elucidates some of the more puzzling aspects of women's opposition to women's rights, it also illuminates how the concept of rights engages women's thinking about moral conflict and choice.

The century marked by the movement for women's rights is spanned roughly by the publication of two novels, both written by women and posing the same moral dilemma, a heroine in love with her cousin Lucy's man. In their parallel triangles these novels provide an historical frame in which to consider the effects of women's rights on women's moral judgments and thus offer a way of addressing the centennial question as to what has changed and what has stayed the same.

In George Eliot's novel *The Mill on the Floss* (1860), Maggie Tulliver "clings to the right." Caught between her love for her cousin Lucy and her "stronger feeling" for Stephen, Lucy's fiancée, Maggie is unswerving in her judgment that, "I must not, cannot, seek my own happiness by sacrificing others." When Stephen says that their love, natural and unsought, makes it "right that we should marry each other," Maggie replies that while "love is natural, surely pity and faithfulness and memory are natural too." Even after "it was too late already not to have caused misery," Maggie refuses to "take a good for myself that has been wrung out of [others'] misery," choosing instead to renounce Stephen and return alone to St. Oggs.

While the minister, Mr. Kenn, considers "the principle upon which she acted as a safer guide than any balancing of consequences," the narrator's judgment is less clear. George Eliot, having placed her heroine in a dilemma that admits no viable resolution, ends the novel by drowning Maggie, but not without first cautioning the reader that "the shifting relation between passion and duty is clear to no man who is capable of apprehending it." Since "the mysterious complexity of our life" cannot be "laced up in formulas," moral judgment cannot be bound by "general rules" but must instead be informed "by a life vivid and intense enough to have created a wide, fellow-feeling with all that is human."

Yet given that in this novel the "eyes of intense life" that were Maggie's look out in the end from a "weary, beaten face," it is not surprising that Margaret Drabble, steeped in the tradition of nineteenth century fiction but engaged in the issues of twentieth century feminism, should choose to return to Eliot's story and explore the possibility of an alternative resolution. In *The Waterfall* (1969) she recreates Maggie's dilemma in *The Mill on the Floss* but, as the title implies, with the difference that the societal impediment has been removed. Thus Drabble's heroine, Jane Grey, clings not to the right but to Lucy's husband, renouncing the renunciations and instead "drowning in the first chapter." Immersed in a sea of self-discovery, "not caring who should drown so long as I should reach the land," Jane is caught by the problem of judgment as she seeks to apprehend the miracle of her survival and to find a way to tell that story. Her love for James, Lucy's husband, is narrated by two different voices, a first and a third person who battle constantly over the issues of judgment and truth, engaging and disengaging the moral questions of responsibility and choice.

Though the balance between passion and duty has shifted between 1860 and 1969, the moral problem remains in both novels the same. Across the intervening century, the verdict of selfishness impales both heroines. The same accusation that compels Maggie's renunciation orchestrates Jane's elaborate plea of helplessness and excuse: "I was merely trying to defend myself against an accusation of selfishness, judge me leniently, I said, I am not as others are, I am sad, I am mad, so I have to have what I want." But the problem with activity and desire that the accusation of selfishness implies not only leads Jane into familiar strategies of evasion and disguise but also impels her to confront the underlying premise on which this accusation is based. Taking apart the moral judgment of the past that had made it seem, "in a sense, better to renounce myself than them," Jane seeks to reconstitute it in a way that could "admit me and encompass me." Thus she strives to create "a new ladder, a new virtue," one that could include activity, sexuality, and survival without abandoning the old virtues of responsibility and care: "If I need to understand what I am doing, if I cannot act without my own approbation—and I must act, I have changed, I am no longer capable of inaction—then I will invent a morality that condones me. Though by doing so, I risk condemning all that I have been."

These novels thus demonstrate the continuing power for women of the judgment of selfishness and the morality of self-abnegation that it implies. This is the judgment that regularly appears at the fulcrum of novels of female adolescence, the turning point of the *Bildungsroman* that separates the invulnerability of childhood innocence from the responsibility of adult participation and choice. The notion that virtue for women lies in self-sacrifice has complicated the course of women's development by pitting the moral issue of goodness against the adult questions of responsibility and choice. In addition, the ethic of self-sacrifice is directly in conflict with the concept of rights that has, in this past century, supported women's claim to a fair share of social justice.

But a further problem arises from the tension between a morality of rights that dissolves "natural bonds" in support of individual claims and a morality of responsibility that knits such claims into a fabric of relationship, blurring the distinction between self and other through the representation of their interdependence. This problem was the concern of Wollstonecraft and Stanton, of Eliot and Drabble. This concern emerged as well in interviews with college women in the 1970s. All of these women talked about the same conflict, all revealed the enormous power of the judgment of selfishness in women's thought. But the appearance of this judgment in the moral conflicts described by contemporary women brings into focus the role that the concept of rights plays in women's moral development. These conflicts demonstrate the continuation through time of an ethic of responsibility as the center of women's moral concern, anchoring the self in a world of relationships and giving rise to activities of care, but also indicate how this ethic is transformed by the recognition of the justice of the rights approach.

The senior year interview with Nan, one of the women in the college student study, illustrates some of the dimensions of women's moral concern in 1973, the year that the Supreme Court decided that abortion is legal and that women have the right to choose whether or not to continue a pregnancy. Two years before, Nan chose to take a course on moral and political choice because she was "looking for different ways of thinking about things" and was interested "in arguments that protect individual freedom." Claiming to "suffer from a low self-image," she reports, in her senior year, a sense of moral progress and growth which she attributes to having had "to review a lot of what I thought about myself" as a result of having become pregnant and deciding to have an abortion. Attributing the pregnancy to "a lapse of self-control, decision-making, and very much stupidity," she considered abortion to be a desperate and life-saving solution ("I felt very much to save my own life that I had to do it"), but one which she viewed as, "at least in the eyes of society, if not my own, a moral sin."

Given her "personal feeling of being very evil," her discovery that "people would help me out anyway did great things for my feelings toward them and myself." In the month that she spent waiting and thinking about the abortion, she thought "a lot about decision-making, and for the first time I wanted to take control of and responsibility for my own decisions in life." As a result, her self-image changed:

> Because now that you are going to take control of your life, you don't feel like you are a pawn in other people's hands. You have to accept the fact that you have done something wrong, and it also gives you a little more integrity, because you are not fighting off these things in yourself all the time. A lot of conflicts are resolved, and you have a sense of a new beginning, based on a kind of conviction that you can act in a situation.

Thus she "came out basically supporting myself, not as a good or bad human being, but simply as a human being who had a lot to learn either way." Seeing herself in the present as capable of choice, she feels responsible for herself in a new way. But while the experience of choice has led Nan to a greater sense of personal integrity, her judgment of these choices stays remarkably the same. Although she has come to a more inclusive and tolerant understanding of herself and a new conception of relationships that will, she believes, allow her to be "more obvious with myself and more independent," the moral issue remains one of responsibility.

In this sense, she considers the pregnancy to have "come to my aid" in illuminating her previous failure to take responsibility:

> It was so serious that it brought to light things in myself, like feelings about myself, my feelings about the world. What I had done, I felt, was so wrong that it came to light to me that I was not taking responsibility where I could have, and I could have gone on like I was, not taking responsibility. So the seriousness of the situation brings the questions right up in front of your face. You see them very clearly, and then the answers are there for you.

Seeing her own irresponsibility as having led to a situation in which she could envision no way of acting that would not cause hurt, she begins "getting rid of old ideas" about morality that now seem an impediment to her goal of living in a way that will not "cause human suffering." In doing so, she calls into question the opposition of selfishness and morality, discerning that "the word *selfish* is tricky." Recognizing that "individual freedom" is not "all that incompatible with morality," she expands her conception of morality, defining it as "the sense of concern for another human being and your sense of concern for yourself." While the moral questions remain, "How much suffering are you going to cause?" and "Why do you have the right to cause human suffering?" these questions apply not only to others but also to herself. Responsibility, separated from self-sacrifice, becomes tied instead to the understanding of the causes of suffering and the ability to anticipate which actions are likely to eventuate in hurt.

The right to include oneself in the compass of a morality of responsibility was a critical question for college women in the 1970s. This question, which arose in differing contexts, posed a problem of inclusion that could be resolved through the logic of justice, the fairness of equating other and self. But it also posed a problem of relationships, whose solution required a new understanding of responsibility and care. Hilary, explaining at age twenty-seven how her thinking about morality has changed, describes her understanding of morality at the time she entered college:

> I was much more simple-minded then. I went through a period in which I thought there were fairly simple answers to questions of right and wrong in life. I even went through a period that now strikes me as so simplistic: I thought that as long as I didn't hurt anybody, everything would be fine. And I soon figured out, or eventually figured out, that things were not that simple, that you were bound to hurt people, they were bound to hurt you, and life is full of tension and conflict. People are bound to hurt each other's feelings, intentionally, unintentionally, but just in the very way things are. So I abandoned that idea.

This abandonment occurred in her first years of college:

> I became involved in a love affair with a guy who wanted to settle down and get married, and I could not imagine a worse

fate, but I was really quite fond of him. And we broke up, and he was so upset by it that he left school for a year, and I realized that I had hurt him very badly and that I hadn't meant to, and I had violated my first principle of moral behavior, but I had made the right decision.

Explaining that she "could not have possibly married him," Hilary felt that there was, in that sense, an "easy answer" to the dilemma she faced. Yet, in another sense, given her moral injunction against hurting, the situation presented an insoluble problem, allowing no course of action that would not eventuate in hurt. This realization led her to question her former absolute moral injunction and to "figure that this principle [of not hurting] was not all there was to it." The limitation she saw pertained directly to the issue of personal integrity; "What that principle was not even attempting to achieve was, 'To thine own self be true.' " Indicating that she had started to think more about maintaining her personal integrity, she says that this experience led her to conclude that, "You can't worry about not hurting other people; just do what is right for you."

Yet, in view of her continuing equation of morality with caring for others and her continuing belief that "acts that are self-sacrificing and that are done for other people or for the good of humanity are good acts," her abandonment of the principle of not hurting others was tantamount to an abandonment of moral concern. Recognizing the rightness of her decision but also realizing its painful consequences, she can see no way to maintain her integrity while adhering to an ethic of care in relationships. Seeking to avoid conflict and compromise in choice by "just doing what is right for you," she is in fact left with a feeling of compromise about herself.

This feeling is apparent as she recounts the dilemma that she faced in her work as a lawyer when opposing counsel in a trial overlooked a document that provided critical support for his client's "meritorious claim." Deliberating whether or not to tell her opponent of the document that would help his client's case, Hilary realized that the adversary system of justice impedes not only "the supposed search for truth" but also the expression of concern for the person on the other side. Choosing in the end to adhere to the system, in part because of the vulnerability of her own professional position, she sees herself as having failed to live up to her standard of personal integrity as well as to her moral ideal of self-sacrifice. Thus her description of herself contrasts both with her depiction of her husband as "a person of absolute integrity who would never do anything he didn't feel was right" and with her view of her mother as "a very caring person" who is "selfless" in giving to others.

On her own behalf, Hilary says somewhat apologetically that she has become, since college, more tolerant and more understanding, less ready to blame people whom formerly she would have condemned, more capable of seeing the integrity of different perspectives. Though she has access, as a lawyer, to the language of rights and recognizes clearly the importance of self-determination and respect, the concept of rights remains in tension with an ethic of care. The continuing opposition of selfishness and responsibility, however, leaves her no way to reconcile the injunction to be true to herself with the ideal of responsibility in relationships.

The clash between a morality of rights and an ethic of responsibility erupted in a moral crisis described by Jenny, another student in the college study. She also articulates a morality of selflessness and self-sacrificing behavior, exemplified by her mother who represents her ideal.

> If I could grow up to be like anyone in the world, it would be my mother, because I've just never met such a selfless person. She would do anything for anybody, up to a point that she has hurt herself a lot because she just gives so much to other people and asks nothing in return. So, ideally, that's what you'd like to be, a person who is selfless and giving.

In contrast, Jenny describes herself as "much more selfish in a lot of ways." But seeing the limitation of self-sacrifice in its potential to hurt others who are close to the self, she seeks to resolve the tension between selfishness and care, revising her definition of "the best person you could possibly be" by adding to its basic component, "doing the most good for other people," the qualification "while fulfilling your own potentialities."

Two years earlier, in the course on moral and political choice, Jenny had set out to examine morality in terms of the questions, "How much do you owe yourself?" and "How much do you owe other people?" Defining morality as a problem of obligation, she attempted, through the equation of self and others, to challenge the premises underlying self-sacrifice and to align her conception of responsibility with an understanding of rights. But a crisis that occurred in her family at that time called into question the logic of this endeavor by demonstrating the inadequacy of the rights terminology to deal with the issues of responsibility in relationships. The crisis was caused by the suicide of a relative at a time when the resources of the family already were strained by the illness of her grandfather, who was in need of continual care. Although the morality of suicide had been discussed in the course from the perspective of individual rights, this suicide appeared instead to Jenny as an act of consummate irresponsibility, increasing the burden of care for others and adding further suffering and hurt.

Trying to bring her feelings of rage into connection with her logic of reason, she reached an impasse in the discovery that her old way of thinking did not work anymore:

> The whole semester we had been discussing what's right and what's wrong, what's good, and how much do you owe yourself and how much do you owe other people, and then my [relative] killed himself, right then, and that's a moral crisis, right? And I didn't know how to handle it because I really ended up hating him for having done that, and I knew I really couldn't do this. I mean, that was wrong, but how could he do this to his family? And I really had to seriously reevaluate that whole course because it just didn't work anymore. All these nice little things that we had been discussing are fine when you talk about it. I remember, we had little stories, like, if you were on a mission and were leading a patrol and somebody had to go and throw a hand grenade or something. Well, that's fine, but when it's something like this that's close to you, it just doesn't work anymore. And I had to seriously reevaluate everything I had said in that course and why, if I believed all that, I could end up with such an intense hatred?

Given the awesome dimensions of this problem, the underlying logic of the equation of how much is owed to oneself versus others began to unravel and then fall apart.

> All of a sudden, all the definitions and all the terminology just fell apart. It became the type of thing that you could not place any value on it to say, "Yes, it was moral," or "No, it was not." It's one of those things that is just irrational and undefinable.

Jenny realized that whatever the judgment, the action itself was irreversible and had consequences that affected the lives of others as well. Since rights and responsibilities, selfishness and self-sacrifice, were so inextricably confounded in this situation, she could find no way of thinking about it except to say that, while in one sense it seemed a moral crisis, in another it appeared "just irrational and undefinable."

Five years later, when interviewed again, Jenny says that these events changed her life by bringing into focus for her "the whole thing about responsibility." When the opposition between selfishness and morality prevailed, she was responsive neither to others nor to herself; not wanting "to take responsibility for her grandfather," she also did not want to take responsibility for herself. Having been, in this sense, both selfish and selfless, she saw the limitation of the opposition itself. Realizing that "it was too easy to go through life the way I had done, letting someone else take responsibility for the direction of my life," she challenged herself to take control and "changed the direction of my life."

The underlying construction of morality as a problem of responsibility and the struggle for women in taking responsibility for their own lives are evident in the dilemmas described by other college students who took part in the rights and responsibilities study. A comparison of the dilemmas described by three of the women shows, across a wide range of formulations, how the opposition between selfishness and responsibility complicates for women the issue of choice, leaving them suspended between an ideal of selflessness and the truth of their own agency and needs. The developmental problem created by the opposition between morality and truth is apparent in the attempt of all three women to find a way to overcome this opposition, to be more honest with themselves while remaining responsive to others. Searching for a way to resolve the tension they feel between responsibilities to others and self-development, they all describe dilemmas that center on the conflict between personal integrity and loyalty in family relationships. All three women have difficulty with choice and tie their difficulty to their wish not to cause hurt. Their various resolutions of this problem reveal, successively, the self-blinding nature of the opposition between selfishness and responsibility, the challenge of the concept of rights to the virtue of selflessness, and the way in which an understanding of rights transforms the understanding of care and relationships.

Alison, a sophomore, defines morality as a consciousness of power:

> A type of consciousness, a sensitivity to humanity, that you can affect someone else's life, you can affect your own life, and you have a responsibility not to endanger other people's lives or to hurt other people. So morality is complex; I'm being very simplistic. Morality involves realizing that there is an interplay between self and other and that you are going to have to take responsibility for both of them. I keep using that word *responsibility*; it's just sort of a consciousness of your influence over what's going on.

Tying morality to an awareness of power but equating responsibility with not hurting others, Alison considers responsibility to mean "that you care about that other person, that you are sensitive to that other person's needs and you consider them as a part of your needs because you are dependent on other people." The equation of morality with caring for others leads her to name "selfishness" as the opposite of responsibility, an opposition manifest in her judgment that the experience of personal gratification compromises the morality of acts that otherwise would be considered responsible and good: "Tutoring was almost a selfish thing because it made me feel good to do something for others and I enjoyed it."

Thus morality, though seen as arising from the interplay between self and others, is reduced to an opposition between self and other, tied in the end to dependence on others and equated with responsibility to care for them. The moral ideal is not cooperation or interdependence but rather the fulfillment of an obligation, the repayment of a debt, by giving to others without taking anything for oneself. The blinding quality of this construction is evident, however, as Alison begins her description of herself, saying, "I am not very honest with myself." The source of this dishonesty lies in the need for self-deception created by an apparent contradiction in her view of herself:

> I am a person who has a lot of ideas about the way I would like things to be and who wants, just through love, to make everything better, but also I am a selfish person, and a lot of the time I don't behave in a loving manner.

In an effort to deal with the problem of selfishness, Alison experiences a continuing struggle "to justify my actions" as well as "a hard time making choices." Seeing that she has the power to hurt but wishing to do none, she has difficulty telling her parents that she wants to take a year off from school, since she knows that her staying at college is important to them. Caught between the wish not to hurt others and the wish to be true to herself, she tries to clarify her own motivation in an attempt to act in a way that is beyond reproach. Striving "to be honest with myself about why I am unhappy here, what is going on, what I want to do," she finds she has difficulty explaining to herself as well as to her parents "why I really have to take the year off, why it's really important to me." Seeing college as a "selfish" institution where competition overrides cooperation, so that "working for yourself, doing for yourself, you don't help other people," she aspires to be "caring, sensitive, and giving," engaged in cooperative rather than competitive relationships. But she can see no way in the complication of this situation to integrate an ideal of personal and moral integrity with an ethic of responsibility and care, since in leaving college, she would hurt her parents, while in staying, she hurts herself. The tension is evident as she describes her wish to be both honest and caring, "someone who is committed to certain ideas but is able to relate to other people and to respect other people's ideas and yet not compromise and not be just submissive and accommodate to other people."

Emily, the second woman, clarifies how this struggle engages the notion of rights. When asked, as a college senior, if she has ever faced a decision where the moral principle is not clear, she describes her conflict with her parents over where she should go to medical school the following year. Explaining her parents' position, that she should not go far away, she sets up a contrast between moral and selfish justifications:

> They had moral justifications of principle and justifications for wanting me here that were both good and not so good. The good ones I can put in the classification of morals, and the bad ones in the classification of selfishness.

Casting the dilemma in the language of rights, she explains:

> My parents have a right to want to see me a certain way, at certain times. I think the bad part was sort of the abuse of that

right, which kind of brings up the selfishness issue and my moral part, which was that I didn't view my going away as breaking up the family in any sense.

Equating rights with wants and morality with responsibility in relationships, she indicates that it was not her "aim or goal to break up the family." Rather, "I thought and I still think in some respects that I would grow more by being in a different place with different people." Contrasting the "positive aspect of separation," her attempt to take responsibility for her own growth, with "the negative on my side," the fact that her parents would be hurt, she encounters a problem of interpretation. The old moral language returns but immediately becomes relativized as she describes her own position:

My motivation was sort of selfish in part or not high enough. Our family was not only a given but sort of a life-long given, and it was sort of my moral obligation, all things being relative, equally to accept that aspect of not going, to be staying here, and I was letting some of my unselfishness take control of the situation.

Her emerging sense that selfishness and unselfishness might be relative rather than absolute judgments, a matter of interpretation or perspective rather than of truth, extends into two concepts of morality, one centered on rights, the other on responsibility. The shift between these two concepts is evident as she defines the moral conflict she faced:

The conflict was whether or not I had the right to act as an independent party when I did not see my leaving as doing harm to other parties but just being a zero. They, on their part, saw it as a negative, although I did not perceive it that way. The conflict was not in my interpretation but in the fact that we had different interpretations of that morality, and it was very close in that I thought both interpretations were relatively equally stacked, and I guess I opted for theirs by staying here, and I guess that was the conflict.

Before, Emily had thought that there is "always one moral position, one higher, and that higher can be a quarter of one percent.

I do believe that it is possible to closely match things out." In this situation, however, she found that it is "impossible to make a moral decision." Having justified her right to act as an independent party in terms of her belief that in doing so she would not hurt others, she nevertheless acceded in the end to her parents' interpretation that her leaving would be selfish since they would be hurt. In explaining the "critical reason" for her decision to stay, she describes how she constructed the dilemma as a balance of selfishness and concluded that hers was "the greater selfishness":

> They were really, really hurt by the whole situation, and I didn't feel the loss so greatly, not going. So I guess I began to view my selfishness as more than their selfishness. Both selfishnesses started out being equal, but somehow or other they appeared to be suffering more.

Thus the rights construction, itself cast in the language of responsibility as a balance of selfishness, in the end gave way to considerations of responsibility, the question of who would suffer more. The attempt to set up the dilemma as a conflict of rights turned it into a contest of selfishnesses, precluding the possibility of a moral decision, since either resolution could be construed as selfish from one or the other perspective. Consequently, the concern with rights was overridden by a concern with responsibility, and she resolved the dilemma by "letting some of my unselfishness take control," since she saw her parents as more vulnerable than herself.

Dismissing the hurt to herself as one of omission ("not having a new experience is not a hurt in the absolute sense"), she contrasts it with the act of commission, the responsibility she would feel for causing her parents "a fairly great loss." Considering responsibility to be "attached to morality," she sees responsibilities as setting up "a chain of expectations, and if you interrupt that, you interrupt a whole process for not only yourself but all those around you." As a result, considerations of rights, based on an assumption of independence, threaten to interrupt the chain of relationships and thus are counterbalanced and outweighed by considerations of responsibility. In the end, choice hinges on the determination of where "the greater responsibility lies," a determination based on an assessment of vulnerability, a relative estimate of who will be more hurt.

However, in relinquishing her "right to act as an independent party" and instead letting her "unselfishness take control," she has suspended her own interpretation of a morality of responsibility, and suspending her interpretations, she suspends herself. This feeling of suspension is caught in Emily's description of herself as "a little round jelly bean, sort of wandering around, picking up snow here and there, never really sinking with the weight of the snow." Toward the end of the interview she indicates her wish to anchor herself more securely by becoming more "thoughtful" about her relationships, more concerned with knowing how she is "interacting with people" rather than just "letting it ride." Whereas previously she was "kind of defensive and afraid" to think about what she was doing in relationships, she nows sees that "thinking about it has taken away that fear, because when you think about what you are doing, you know what it is. If you don't know, you just kind of let it ride; you don't know what is going to come next."

The image of drifting along or riding it out recurs throughout the interviews to denote the experience of women caught in the opposition between selfishness and responsibility. Describing a life lived in response, guided by the perception of others' needs, they can see no way of exercising control without risking an assertion that seems selfish and hence morally dangerous. Like the heroine of *The Waterfall,* who begins the novel by saying, "If I were drowning I couldn't reach out a hand to save myself, so unwilling am I to set myself up against fate," without even thinking "that it might be the truth," these women are drawn unthinkingly by the image of passivity, the appeal of avoiding responsibility by sinking, like Jane, into an "ice age of inactivity," so that "providence could deal with her without her own assistance."

But the image of drifting, while seeming to offer safety from the onus of responsibility, carries with it the danger of landing in a more painful confrontation with choice, as in the stark alternatives of an abortion decision, or in Maggie Tulliver's realization that she had unwittingly done the thing she most feared. Then in the recognition of consequence, the issue of responsibility returns, bringing with it the related questions of choice and of truth.

Maggie, giving in to her feelings for Stephen by momentarily ceasing her resistance to him,

> felt that she was being led down the garden among the roses, being helped with firm tender care into the boat, having the cushion and cloak arranged for her feet and her parasol opened for her (which she had forgotten)—all by this stronger

presence that seemed to bear her along without any act of her own will.

But when she realized how far they had gone, "a terrible alarm took possession of her," and her "yearning after that belief that the tide was doing it all" quickly gave way, first to "feelings of angry resistance toward Stephen," whom she accused of having wanted to deprive her of choice and having taken advantage of her thoughtlessness, but then to the realization of her own participation. No longer "paralyzed," she recognized that "the feelings of a few short weeks had hurried her into the sins that her nature had most recoiled from: breach of faith and cruel selfishness." Then Maggie, "longing after perfect goodness," chooses "to be true to my calmer affections and live without the joy of love."

However, while Maggie longs for goodness, her counterpart Jane searches for truth. Discovering in her desire for James "such depths of selfishness" that she considers drowning herself "in an effort to reclaim lost renunciations like Maggie Tulliver," Jane chooses instead to question the renunciations and in the end to "identify myself with love." Observing that although "Maggie Tulliver never slept with her man, she did all the damage there was to be done, to Lucy, to herself, to the two men who loved her, and then, like a woman of another age she refrained," Jane confronts "an event seen from angles where there used to be one event and one way only of enduring it." Consequently she "wonders, in this age, what is to be done?"

The moral distinction between selfish and selfless behavior, which became increasingly clear to Maggie, thus becomes for Jane increasingly blurred. Having "sought virtue" only to find that she "could not ascend by the steps that others seemed to take," she then sought innocence "in abnegation, in denial, in renunciation," thinking that,

> if I could deny myself enough I would achieve some kind of innocence, despite those intermittent nightmare promptings of my true nature. I thought I could negate myself and wipe myself out.

Yet she discovers that, no matter which way she tells the story, whether in the first or the third person, in the end she confronts the truth that despite all the renunciations, she has "drowned in a willing sea."

It is against the pull of such renunciations, the vision of an innocence attained by the denial of self, that women begin to search for the truth of their own experience and to talk of taking control.

> (*Thinking back over the past year, what stands out for you?*)
> Taking control of my life.

Thus Kate, the third woman and a recent college graduate, begins to tell of her struggle to overcome the opposition between selfishness and responsibility and to take control of her life. The struggle erupted in her senior year when she found herself unable to enact her wish to leave a varsity team in order to do "other things that were important to me." In contemplating the radical act of saying no to the "unquestioned past priority" of sports in her life, she found herself "paralyzed in a way" and unable to make a decision:

> I just was having a hard time. The decision was very difficult. It was like I couldn't make it, I was just stuck. And I would try to think about it, and it was just like coming up against a wall, even trying to figure out why it was so difficult and why I was having such a hard time. So finally it turned into a little bit of a crisis situation in that the coach said to me, "Look, you have to decide, one way or the other," and I just didn't feel like I could decide. Things had gotten really messy in terms of emotions and everything. So for the first time, significantly, that I can think of, I admitted that I was having big troubles.

Her troubles stemmed from the fact that, in saying no, she was challenging a "whole ethic" that previously had been unquestioned. Having grown up thinking of the world view represented by her father—"succeeding in whatever you do and the sports ethic"—as "the only legitimate one," she now realized "how basic a thing it had become in terms of being an attitude I lived by." Thus in finding that "there were other things that were more important to me," she posed "a real threat or a real challenge to one of the root assumptions that I had been living by for a long time," an assumption that had been an anchor of her identity and a bond between her father and herself.

Describing herself as previously having "floated" through school with "such a nonexistent sense of what I wanted to do that I kind of went the path of least resistance," Kate has taken control by "more and more doing what I want to do and less and less what I thought I should be doing or was supposed to be doing." In this way, she has become "more embedded in where I am." Recognizing the legitimacy of different world views, she relies more on her own interpretations. Thus the process of taking control, of coming "to a more defined sense of what I wanted to do and what options are available and what kinds of paths make sense," took on new meaning:

> It meant coming into myself a little bit, and so becoming more confident in my own judgment, because I had something to base my judgments on; feeling stronger in myself and so relying more on myself to make decisions and to evaluate situations; and not accepting my parents' judgments or [college's] judgments; and finding myself in situations where I was taking one position and someone else was taking another position and both positions seemed legitimate and neither was *the* right one, and learning how to accept that; and trying to figure out why that was, but being able to accept that, or starting to, or starting to question that whole idea that one person is more right than the other or doing it better than the other.

In starting to question the idea that there is a single right way to live and that differences are always a matter of better and worse, she began to see conflict in a new way, as a part of rather than a threat to relationships. Contrasting her current thinking about morality with her previous belief that "there were right answers," she refers to a course on moral development that she had taken in her sophomore year:

> The idea that at the highest level of moral reasoning, you get a group of people together on a problem and, ideally, they should all agree made sense to me. It was amazing to me, although it was very confusing. It was so clean. It is so clean, that idea that there are right answers, that everyone will reach the right answers.

Since the notion of agreement was premised on the concept of rights, it tied in with Kate's understanding of feminism at that time

The recognition of women's rights "legitimized a lot of the grumblings and dissatisfactions that I had for what I felt were women's choices." Similarly, the equation of morality with respect for rights justified the freedom of choice she sought, placing bounds on responsibility by limiting duty to the reciprocity of noninterference Now, however, she sees the limitation of the "individually-centered" approach of balancing rights and claims in the failure of this approach to take into account the reality of relationships, "a whole other dimension to human experience." In seeing individual lives as connected and embedded in a social context of relationship, she expands her moral perspective to encompass a notion of "collective life." Responsibility now includes both self and other, viewed as different but connected rather than as separate and opposed. This cognizance of interdependence, rather than a concern with reciprocity, informs her belief that "we all do to some extent have responsibilities to look out for each other."

Since moral problems arise in situations of conflict where "either way I go, something or someone will not be served," their resolution is "not just a simple yes or no decision; it is worse." In a world that extends through an elaborate network of relationships, the fact that someone is hurt affects everyone who is involved, complicating the morality of any decision and removing the possibility of a clear or simple solution. Thus morality, rather than being opposed to integrity or tied to an ideal of agreement, is aligned with "the kind of integrity" that comes from "making decisions after working through everything you think is involved and important in the situation," and taking responsibility for choice. In the end, morality is a matter of care:

> It is taking the time and energy to consider everything. To decide carelessly or quickly or on the basis of one or two factors when you know that there are other things that are important and that will be affected, that's immoral. The moral way to make decisions is by considering as much as you possibly can, as much as you know.

Describing herself as "a strong person," though acknowledging that she does not always feel strong, Kate sees herself as "thoughtful and careful," as "painfully starting to learn how to express myself and be more open," rather than taking, as before, a "stoic attitude." While her participation in sports led her to "take myself seriously physically," her involvement in feminism led her to take her ideas and feelings seriously as well. More responsive now to herself and more directly responsive to others as well, she describes a morality that includes the logic of rights in a new understanding of responsibility. Seeing life not as "a path" but "a web, where you can choose different paths at any particular time, so it's not like there is just one way," she realizes that there will always be conflict and that "no factor is absolute." The only "real constant is the process" of making decisions with care, on the basis of what you know, and taking responsibility for choice while seeing the possible legitimacy of other solutions.

In equating responsibility with caring rather than with not hurting, Kate recognizes the problem of limitation: "We do have responsibilities to each other in terms of helping other people—I don't know how far." Although inclusion is the goal of moral consciousness, exclusion may be a necessity of life. The people whom she admires are "people who are really connected to the concrete situations in their life," whose knowledge comes not from detachment but from living in connection with themselves and with others, from being embedded in the conditions of life.

In one sense, then, not much has changed. George Eliot, observing that "we have no master-key that will fit all cases" of moral decision, returns to the casuists in whose "perverted spirit of minute discrimination" she sees "the shadow of a truth to which eyes and hearts are too often fatally sealed—the truth that moral judgments must remain false and hollow unless they are checked and enlightened by a perpetual reference to the special circumstances that mark the individual lot." Thus moral judgment must be informed by "growing insight and sympathy," tempered by the knowledge gained through experience that "general rules" will not lead people "to justice by a ready-made patent method, without the trouble of exerting patience, discrimination, impartiality, without any care to assure whether they have the insight that comes from a hardly-earned estimate of temptation or from a life vivid and intense enough to have created a wide, fellow feeling with all that is human."

And yet, for Eliot, at least in this novel, the moral problem remains one of renunciation, a question of "whether the moment has come in which a man has fallen below the possibility of a renunciation that will carry any efficacy, and must accept the sway of a passion against which he had struggled as a trespass.'' The opposition of passion and duty thus binds morality to an ideal of selflessness, the "perfect goodness" toward which Maggie Tulliver aspired.

Both this opposition and this ideal are called into question by the concept of rights, by the assumption underlying the idea of justice that self and other are equal. Among college students in the 1970s, the concept of rights entered into their thinking to challenge a morality of self-sacrifice and self-abnegation. Questioning the stoicism of self-denial and replacing the illusion of innocence with an awareness of choice, they struggled to grasp the essential notion of rights, that the interests of the self can be considered legitimate. In this sense, the concept of rights changes women's conceptions of self, allowing them to see themselves as stronger and to consider directly their own needs. When assertion no longer seems dangerous, the concept of relationships changes from a bond of continuing dependence to a dynamic of interdependence. Then the notion of care expands from the paralyzing injunction not to hurt others to an injunction to act responsively toward self and others and thus to sustain connection. A consciousness of the dynamics of human relationships then becomes central to moral understanding, joining the heart and the eye in an ethic that ties the activity of thought to the activity of care.

Thus changes in women's rights change women's moral judgments, seasoning mercy with justice by enabling women to consider it moral to care not only for others but for themselves. The issue of inclusion first raised by the feminists in the public domain reverberates through the psychology of women as they begin to notice their own exclusion of themselves. When the concern with care extends from an injunction not to hurt others to an ideal of responsibility in social relationships, women begin to see their understanding of relationships as a source of moral strength. But the concept of rights also changes women's moral judgments by adding a second perspective to the consideration of moral problems, with the result that judgment becomes more tolerant and less absolute.

As selfishness and self-sacrifice become matters of interpretation and responsibilities live in tension with rights, moral truth is complicated by psychological truth, and the matter of judgment becomes more complex. Drabble's heroine, who sought to write "a poem as round and hard as a stone," only to find that words and thoughts obtrude, concludes that "a poem so round and smooth would say nothing" and sets out to describe the variegated edges of an event seen from angles, finding in the end no unified truth. Instead, through a final shift in perspective, she relegates her suspicions to "that removed, third person" and, no longer fending off the accusation of selfishness, identifies herself with the first person voice.

6 Visions of Maturity

TTACHMENT AND SEPARATION anchor the cycle of human life, describing the biology of human reproduction and the psychology of human development. The concepts of attachment and separation that depict the nature and sequence of infant development appear in adolescence as identity and intimacy and then in adulthood as love and work. This reiterative counterpoint in human experience, however, when molded into a developmental ordering, tends to disappear in the course of its linear reduction into the equation of development with separation. This disappearance can be traced in part to the focus on child and adolescent development, where progress can readily be charted by measuring the distance between mother and child. The limitation of this rendition is most apparent in the absence of women from accounts of adult development.

Choosing like Virgil to "sing of arms and the man," psychologists describing adulthood have focused on the development of self and work. While the apogee of separation in adolescence is presumed to be followed in adulthood by the return of attachment and care, recent depictions of adult development, in their seamless emergence from studies of men, provide scanty illumination of a life spent in intimate and generative relationships. Daniel Levinson (1978), despite his evident distress about the exclusion of women from his necessarily small sample, sets out on the basis of an all-male study "to create an overarching conception of development that could encompass the diverse biological, psychological and social changes occurring in adult life" (p. 8).

Levinson's conception is informed by the idea of "the Dream," which orders the seasons of a man's life in the same way that Jupiter's prophecy of a glorious destiny steers the course of Aeneas' journey. The Dream about which Levinson writes is also a vision of glorious achievement whose realization or modification will shape the character and life of the man. In the salient relationships in Levinson's analysis, the "mentor" facilitates the realization of the Dream, while the "special woman" is the helpmate who encourages the hero to shape and live out his vision: "As the novice adult tries to separate from his family and pre-adult world, and to enter an adult world, he must form significant relationships with other adults who will facilitate his work on the Dream. Two of the most important figures in this drama are the 'mentor' and the 'special woman' (p. 93).

The significant relationships of early adulthood are thus construed as the means to an end of individual achievement, and these "transitional figures" must be cast off or reconstructed following the realization of success. If in the process, however, they become, like Dido, an impediment to the fulfillment of the Dream, then the relationship must be renounced, "to allow the developmental process" to continue. This process is defined by Levinson explicitly as one of individuation: "throughout the life cycle, but especially in the key transition periods . . . the developmental process of *individuation* is going on." The process refers "to the changes in a person's relationships to himself and to the external world," the relationships that constitute his "Life Structure" (p. 195).

If in the course of "Becoming One's Own Man," this structure is discovered to be flawed and threatens the great expectations of the Dream, then in order to avert "serious Failure or Decline," the man must "break out" to salvage his Dream. This act of breaking out is consummated by a "marker event" of separation, such as "leaving his wife, quitting his job, or moving to another region" (p. 206). Thus the road to mid-life salvation runs through either achievement or separation.

From the array of human experience, Levinson's choice is the same as Virgil's, charting the progress of adult development as an arduous struggle toward a glorious destiny. Like pious Aeneas on his way to found Rome, the men in Levinson's study steady their lives by their devotion to realizing their dream, measuring their progress in terms of their distance from the shores of its promised success. Thus in the stories that Levinson recounts, relationships, whatever their particular intensity, play a relatively subordinate role in the individual drama of adult development.

The focus on work is also apparent in George Vaillant's (1977) account of adaptation to life. The variables that correlate with adult adjustment, like the interview that generates the data, bear predominantly on occupation and call for an expansion of Erikson's stages. Filling in what he sees as "an uncharted period of development" which Erikson left "between the decades of the twenties and forties," Vaillant describes the years of the thirties as the era of "Career Consolidation," the time when the men in his sample sought, "like Shakespeare's soldier, 'the bauble Reputation' " (p. 202). With this analogy to Shakespeare's Rome, the continuity of intimacy and generativity is interrupted to make room for a stage of further individuation and achievement, realized by work and consummated by a success that brings societal recognition.

Erikson's (1950) notion of generativity, however, is changed in the process of this recasting. Conceiving generativity as "the concern in establishing and guiding the next generation," Erikson takes the *"productivity* and *creativity"* of parenthood in its literal or symbolic realization to be a metaphor for an adulthood centered on relationships and devoted to the activity of taking care (p. 267). In Erikson's account, generativity is the central stage of adult development, encompassing "man's relationship to his production as well as to his progeny" (p. 268). In Vaillant's data, this relationship is relegated instead to mid-life.

Asserting that generativity is "not just a stage for making little things grow," Vaillant argues against Erikson's metaphor of parenthood by cautioning that "the world is filled with irresponsible mothers who are marvellous at bearing and loving children up to the age of two and then despair of taking the process further." Generativity, in order to exclude such women, is uprooted from its earthy redolence and redefined as "responsibility for the growth, leadership, and well-being of one's fellow creatures, not just raising crops or children" (p. 202). Thus, the expanse of Erikson's conception is narrowed to development in mid-adulthood and in the process is made more restrictive in its definition of care.

As a result, Vaillant emphasizes the relation of self to society and minimizes attachment to others. In an interview about work, health, stress, death, and a variety of family relationships, Vaillant says to the men in his study that "the hardest question" he will ask is, "Can you describe your wife?" This prefatory caution presumably arose from his experience with this particular sample of men but points to the limits of their adaptation, or perhaps to its psychological expense.

Thus the "models for a healthy life cycle" are men who seem distant in their relationships, finding it difficult to describe their wives, whose importance in their lives they nevertheless acknowledge. The same sense of distance between self and others is evident in Levinson's conclusion that, "In our interviews, friendship was largely noticeable by its absence. As a tentative generalization we would say that close friendship with a man or a woman is rarely experienced by American men." Caught by this impression, Levinson pauses in his discussion of the three "tasks" of adulthood (Building and Modifying the Life Structure, Working on Single Components of the Life Structure, and Becoming More Individuated), to offer an elaboration: "A man may have a wide social network in which he has amicable, 'friendly' relationships with many men and perhaps a few women. In general, however, most men do not have an intimate male friend of the kind that they recall fondly from boyhood or youth. Many men have had casual dating relationships with women, and perhaps a few complex love-sex relationships, but most men have not had an intimate non-sexual friendship with a woman. We need to understand why friendship is so rare, and what consequences this deprivation has for adult life" (p. 335).

Thus, there are studies, on the one hand, that convey a view of adulthood where relationships are subordinated to the ongoing process of individuation and achievement, whose progress, however, is predicated on prior attachments and thought to enhance the capacity for intimacy. On the other hand, there is the observation that among those men whose lives have served as the model for adult development, the capacity for relationships is in some sense diminished and the men are constricted in their emotional expression. Relationships often are cast in the language of achievement, characterized by their success or failure, and impoverished in their affective range:

> At forty-five, Lucky, enjoyed one of the best marriages in the Study, but probably not as perfect as he implied when he

wrote, "You may not believe me when I say we've never had a disagreement, large or small."

The biography of Dr. Carson illustrates his halting passage from identity to intimacy, through career consolidation, and, finally, into the capacity to *care* in its fullest sense ... he had gone through divorce, remarriage, and a shift from research to private practice. His personal metamorphosis had continued. The mousy researcher had become a charming clinician ... suave, untroubled, kindly and in control ... The vibrant energy that had characterized his adolescence had returned ... now his depression was clearly an *affect;* and he was anything but fatigued. In the next breath he confessed, "I'm very highly sexed and that's a problem, too." He then provided me with an exciting narrative as he told me not only of recent romantic entanglements but also of his warm fatherly concern for patients (Vaillant, 1977, pp. 129, 203–206).

The notion that separation leads to attachment and that individuation eventuates in mutuality, while reiterated by both Vaillant and Levinson, is belied by the lives they put forth as support. Similarly, in Erikson's studies of Luther and Gandhi, while the relationship between self and society is achieved in magnificent articulation, both men are compromised in their capacity for intimacy and live at great personal distance from others. Thus Luther in his devotion to Faith, like Gandhi in his devotion to Truth, ignore the people most closely around them while working instead toward the glory of God. These men resemble in remarkable detail pious Aeneas in Virgil's epic, who also overcame the bonds of attachment that impeded the progress of his journey to Rome.

In all these accounts the women are silent, except for the sorrowful voice of Dido who, imploring and threatening Aeneas in vain, in the end silences herself upon his sword. Thus there seems to be a line of development missing from current depictions of adult development, a failure to describe the progression of relationships toward a maturity of interdependence. Though the truth of separation is recognized in most developmental texts, the reality of continuing connection is lost or relegated to the background where the figures of women appear. In this way, the emerging conception of adult development casts a familiar shadow on women's lives, pointing again toward the incompleteness of their separation, depicting them as mired in relationships. For women, the developmental markers of separation and attachment, allocated sequentially to adolescence and adulthood, seem in some sense to be fused. However, while this fusion leaves women at risk in a society that rewards separation, it also points to a more general truth currently obscured in psychological texts.

In young adulthood, when identity and intimacy converge in dilemmas of conflicting commitment, the relationship between self and other is exposed. That this relationship differs in the experience of men and women is a steady theme in the literature on human development and a finding of my research. From the different dynamics of separation and attachment in their gender identity formation through the divergence of identity and intimacy that marks their experience in the adolescent years, male and female voices typically speak of the importance of different truths, the former of the role of separation as it defines and empowers the self, the latter of the ongoing process of attachment that creates and sustains the human community.

Since this dialogue contains the dialectic that creates the tension of human development, the silence of women in the narrative of adult development distorts the conception of its stages and sequence. Thus, I want to restore in part the missing text of women's development, as they describe their conceptions of self and morality in the early adult years. In focusing primarily on the differences between the accounts of women and men, my aim is to enlarge developmental understanding by including the perspectives of both of the sexes. While the judgments considered come from a small and highly educated sample, they elucidate a contrast and make it possible to recognize not only what is missing in women's development but also what is there.

This problem of recognition was illustrated in a literature class at a women's college where the students were discussing the moral dilemma described in the novels of Mary McCarthy and James Joyce:

> I felt caught in a dilemma that was new to me then but which since has become horribly familiar: the trap of adult life, in which you are held, wriggling, powerless to act because you can see both sides. On that occasion, as generally in the future, I compromised.
>
> (*Memories of a Catholic Girlhood*)

I will not serve that in which I no longer believe, whether it calls itself my home, my fatherland or my church: and I will try to express myself in some mode of life or art as freely as I can and as wholly as I can, using for my defense the only arms I allow myself to use—silence, exile and cunning.

(*A Portrait of the Artist as a Young Man*)

Comparing the clarity of Stephen's *non serviam* with Mary McCarthy's "zigzag course," the women were unanimous in their decision that Stephen's was the better choice. Stephen was powerful in his certainty of belief and armed with strategies to avoid confrontation; the shape of his identity was clear and tied to a compelling justification. He had, in any case, taken a stand.

Wishing that they could be more like Stephen, in his clarity of decision and certainty of desire, the women saw themselves instead like Mary McCarthy, helpless, powerless, and constantly compromised. The contrasting images of helplessness and power in their explicit tie to attachment and separation caught the dilemma of the women's development, the conflict between integrity and care. In Stephen's simpler construction, separation seemed the empowering condition of free and full self-expression, while attachment appeared a paralyzing entrapment and caring an inevitable prelude to compromise. To the students, Mary McCarthy's portrayal confirmed their own endorsement of this account.

In the novels, however, contrasting descriptions of the road to adult life appear. For Stephen, leaving childhood means renouncing relationships in order to protect his freedom of self-expression. For Mary, "farewell to childhood" means relinquishing the freedom of self-expression in order to protect others and preserve relationships: "A sense of power and Caeserlike magnanimity filled me I was going to equivocate, not for selfish reasons but in the interests of the community, like a grown-up responsible person" (p. 162). These divergent constructions of identity, in self-expression or in self-sacrifice, create different problems for further development— the former a problem of human connection, and the latter a problem of truth. These seemingly disparate problems, however, are intimately related, since the shrinking from truth creates distance in relationship, and separation removes part of the truth. In the college student study which spanned the years of early adulthood, the men's return from exile and silence parallels the women's return from equivocation, until intimacy and truth converge in the discovery of the connection between integrity and care. Then only a difference in tone reveals what men and women know from the beginning and what they only later discover through experience.

The instant choice of self-deprecation in the preference for Stephen by the women in the English class is matched by a childlike readiness for apology in the women in the college student study. The participants in this study were an unequal number of men and women, representing the distribution of males and females in the class on moral and political choice. At age twenty-seven, the five women in the study all were actively pursuing careers—two in medicine, one in law, one in graduate study, and one as an organizer of labor unions. In the five years following their graduation from college, three had married and one had a child.

When they were asked at age twenty-seven, "How would you describe yourself to yourself?" one of the women refused to reply, but the other four gave as their responses to the interviewer's question:

> This sounds sort of strange, but I think maternal, with all its connotations. I see myself in a nurturing role, maybe not right now, but whenever that might be, as a physician, as a mother... It's hard for me to think of myself without thinking about other people around me that I'm giving to.
>
> (Claire)

> I am fairly hard-working and fairly thorough and fairly responsible, and in terms of weaknesses, I am sometimes hesitant about making decisions and unsure of myself and afraid of doing things and taking responsibility, and I think maybe that is one of the biggest conflicts I have had... The other very important aspect of my life is my husband and trying to make his life easier and trying to help him out.
>
> (Leslie)

> I am a hysteric. I am intense. I am warm. I am very smart about people... I have a lot more soft feelings than hard feelings. I am a lot easier to get to be kind than to get mad. If I had to say one word, and to me it incorporates a lot, *adopted.*
>
> (Erica)

> I have sort of changed a lot. At the point of the last interview [age twenty-two] I felt like I was the kind of person who was

interested in growth and trying hard, and it seems to me that the last couple of years, the not trying is someone who is not growing, and I think that is the thing that bothers me the most, the thing that I keep thinking about, that I am not growing. It's not true, I am, but what seems to be a failure partially is the way that Tom and I broke up. The thing with Tom feels to me like I am not growing ... The thing I am running into lately is that the way I describe myself, my behavior doesn't sometimes come out that way. Like I hurt Tom a lot, and that bothers me. So I am thinking of myself as somebody who tried not to hurt people, but I ended up hurting him a lot, and so that is something that weighs on me, that I am somebody who unintentionally hurts people. Or a feeling, lately, that it is simple to sit down and say what your principles are, what your values are, and what I think about myself, but the way it sort of works out in actuality is sometimes very different. You can say you try not to hurt people, but you might because of things about yourself, or you can say this is my principle, but when the situation comes up, you don't really behave the way you would like ... So I consider myself contradictory and confused.

(Nan)

The fusion of identity and intimacy, noted repeatedly in women's development, is perhaps nowhere more clearly articulated than in these self-descriptions. In response to the request to describe themselves, all of the women describe a relationship, depicting their identity *in* the connection of future mother, present wife, adopted child, or past lover. Similarly, the standard of moral judgment that informs their assessment of self is a standard of relationship, an ethic of nurturance, responsibility, and care. Measuring their strength in the activity of attachment ("giving to," "helping out," "being kind," "not hurting"), these highly successful and achieving women do not mention their academic and professional distinction in the context of describing themselves. If anything, they regard their professional activities as jeopardizing their own sense of themselves, and the conflict they encounter between achievement and care leaves them either divided in judgment or feeling betrayed. Nan explains:

When I first applied to medical school, my feeling was that I was a person who was concerned with other people and being able to care for them in some way or another, and I was running into problems the last few years as far as my being able to give of myself, my time, and what I am doing to other people. And medicine, even though it seems that profession is set up to do exactly that, seems to more or less interfere with your doing it. To me it felt like I wasn't really growing, that I was just treading water, trying to cope with what I was doing that made me very angry in some ways because it wasn't the way that I wanted things to go.

Thus in all of the women's descriptions, identity is defined in a context of relationship and judged by a standard of responsibility and care. Similarly, morality is seen by these women as arising from the experience of connection and conceived as a problem of inclusion rather than one of balancing claims. The underlying assumption that morality stems from attachment is explicitly stated by Claire in her response to Heinz's dilemma of whether or not to steal an overpriced drug in order to save his wife. Explaining why Heinz should steal, she elaborates the view of social reality on which her judgment is based:

> By yourself, there is little sense to things. It is like the sound of one hand clapping, the sound of one man or one woman, there is something lacking. It is the collective that is important to me, and that collective is based on certain guiding principles, one of which is that everybody belongs to it and that you all come from it. You have to love someone else, because while you may not like them, you are inseparable from them. In a way, it is like loving your right hand. *They are part of you;* that other person is part of that giant collection of people that you are connected to.

To this aspiring maternal physician, the sound of one hand clapping does not seem a miraculous transcendence but rather a human absurdity, the illusion of a person standing alone in a reality of interconnection.

For the men, the tone of identity is different, clearer, more direct, more distinct and sharp-edged. Even when disparaging the concept itself, they radiate the confidence of certain truth. Although the world of the self that men describe at times includes "people" and "deep attachments," no particular person or relationship is mentioned, nor is the activity of relationship portrayed in the context of self-description. Replacing the women's verbs of attachment are adjectives of separation—"intelligent," "logical," "imaginative," "honest," sometimes even "arrogant" and "cocky." Thus the male "I" is defined in separation, although the men speak of having "real contacts" and "deep emotions" or otherwise wishing for them.

In a randomly selected half of the sample, men who were situated similarly to the women in occupational and marital position give as their initial responses to the request for self-description:

Logical, compromising, outwardly calm. If it seems like my statements are short and abrupt, it is because of my background and training. Architectural statements have to be very concise and short. Accepting. Those are all on an emotional level. I consider myself educated, reasonably intelligent.

I would describe myself as an enthusiastic, passionate person who is slightly arrogant. Concerned, committed, very tired right now because I didn't get much sleep last night.

I would describe myself as a person who is well developed intellectually and emotionally. Relatively narrow circle of friends, acquaintances, persons with whom I have real contacts as opposed to professional contacts or community contacts. And relatively proud of the intellectual skills and development, content with the emotional development as such, as a not very actively pursued goal. Desiring to broaden that one, the emotional aspect.

Intelligent, perceptive—I am being brutally honest now—still somewhat reserved, unrealistic about a number of social situations which involve other people, particularly authorities. Improving, looser, less tense and hung up than I used to be. Somewhat lazy, although it is hard to say how much of that is tied up with other conflicts. Imaginative, sometimes too much so. A little dilletantish, interested in a lot of things without necessarily going into them in depth, although I am moving toward correcting that.

I would tend to describe myself first by recounting a personal history, where I was born, grew up, and that kind of thing, but I am dissatisfied with that, having done it thousands of times. It doesn't seem to capture the essence of what I am, I would probably decide after another futile attempt, because there is no such thing as the essence of what I am, and be very bored by the whole thing . . . I don't think that there is any such thing as myself. There is myself sitting here, there is myself tomorrow, and so on.

Evolving and honest.

I guess on the surface I seem a little easy-going and laid back, but I think I am probably a bit more wound up than that. I tend to get wound up very easily. Kind of smart aleck, a little bit, or cocky maybe. Not as thorough as I should be. A little bit hard-ass, I guess, and a guy that is not swayed by emotions and feelings. I have deep emotions, but I am not a person who has a lot of different people. I have attachments to a few people, very deep attachments. Or attachments to a lot of things, at least in the demonstrable sense.

I guess I think I am kind of creative and also a little bit schizophrenic . . . A lot of it is a result of how I grew up. There is a kind of longing for the pastoral life and, at the same time, a desire for the flash, prestige, and recognition that you get by going out and hustling.

Two of the men begin more tentatively by talking about people in general, but they return in the end to great ideas or a need for distinctive achievement:

I think I am basically a decent person. I think I like people a lot and I like liking people. I like doing things with pleasure from just people, from their existence, almost. Even people I don't know well. When I said I was a decent person, I think that is almost the thing that makes me a decent person, that is a decent quality, a good quality. I think I am very bright. I think I am a little lost, not acting quite like I am inspired— whether it is just a question of lack of inspiration, I don't know—but not accomplishing things, not achieving things,

and not knowing where I want to go or what I'm doing. I
think most people especially doctors, have some idea of what
they are going to be doing in four years. I [an intern] really
have a blank . . . I have great ideas . . . but I can't imagine me
in them.

I guess the things that I like to think are important to me are I
am aware of what is going on around me, other people's needs
around me, and the fact that I enjoy doing things for other
people and I feel good about it. I suppose it's nice in my situation, but I am not sure that is true for everybody. I think some
people do things for other people and it doesn't make them
feel good. Once in awhile that is true of me too, for instance
working around the house, and I am always doing the same
old things that everyone else is doing and eventually I build
up some resentment toward that.

In these men's descriptions of self, involvement with others is tied
to a qualification of identity rather than to its realization. Instead of
attachment, individual achievement rivets the male imagination,
and great ideas or distinctive activity defines the standard of self-
assessment and success.

Thus the sequential ordering of identity and intimacy in the
transition from adolescence to adulthood better fits the development of men than it does the development of women. Power and
separation secure the man in an identity achieved through work,
but they leave him at a distance from others, who seem in some
sense out of his sight. Cranly, urging Stephen Daedalus to perform
his Easter duty for his mother's sake, reminds him:

Your mother must have gone through a good deal of suffering
. . . Would you not try to save her from suffering more even
if—or would you?
If I could, Stephen said, that would cost me very little.

Given this distance, intimacy becomes the critical experience that
brings the self back into connection with others, making it possible
to see both sides—to discover the effects of actions on others as well
as their cost to the self. The experience of relationship brings an
end to isolation, which otherwise hardens into indifference, an absence of active concern for others, though perhaps a willingness to
respect their rights. For this reason, intimacy is the transformative

experience for men through which adolescent identity turns into the generativity of adult love and work. In the process, as Erikson (1964) observes, the knowledge gained through intimacy changes the ideological morality of adolescence into the adult ethic of taking care.

Since women, however, define their identity through relationships of intimacy and care, the moral problems that they encounter pertain to issues of a different sort. When relationships are secured by masking desire and conflict is avoided by equivocation, then confusion arises about the locus of responsibility and truth. McCarthy, describing her "representations" to her grandparents, explains:

> Whatever I told them was usually so blurred and glossed, in the effort to meet their approval (for, aside from anything else, I was fond of them and tried to accommodate myself to their perspective), that except when answering a direct question, I hardly knew whether what I was saying was true or false. I really tried, or so I thought, to avoid lying, but it seemed to me that they forced it on me by the difference in their vision of things, so that I was always transposing reality for them into terms they could understand. To keep matters straight with my conscience, I shrank, whenever possible, from the lie absolute, just as, from a sense of precaution, I shrank from the plain truth.

The critical experience then becomes not intimacy but choice, creating an encounter with self that clarifies the understanding of responsibility and truth.

Thus in the transition from adolescence to adulthood, the dilemma itself is the same for both sexes, a conflict between integrity and care. But approached from different perspectives, this dilemma generates the recognition of opposite truths. These different perspectives are reflected in two different moral ideologies, since separation is justified by an ethic of rights while attachment is supported by an ethic of care

The morality of rights is predicated on equality and centered on the understanding of fairness, while the ethic of responsibility relies on the concept of equity, the recognition of differences in need While the ethic of rights is a manifestation of equal respect, balancing the claims of other and self, the ethic of responsibility rests on an understanding that gives rise to compassion and care. Thus the counterpoint of identity and intimacy that marks the time between childhood and adulthood is articulated through two different moralities whose complementarity is the discovery of maturity.

The discovery of this complementarity is traced in the study by questions about personal experiences of moral conflict and choice. Two lawyers chosen from the sample illustrate how the divergence in judgment between the sexes is resolved through the discovery by each of the other's perspective and of the relationship between integrity and care.

The dilemma of responsibility and truth that McCarthy describes is reiterated by Hilary, a lawyer and the woman who said she found it too hard to describe herself at the end of what "really has been a rough week." She too, like McCarthy, considers self-sacrificing acts "courageous" and "praiseworthy," explaining that "if everyone on earth behaved in a way that showed care for others and courage, the world would be a much better place, you wouldn't have crime and you might not have poverty." However, this moral ideal of self-sacrifice and care ran into trouble not only in a relationship where the conflicting truths of each person's feelings made it impossible to avoid hurt, but also in court where, despite her concern for the client on the other side, she decided not to help her opponent win his case.

In both instances, she found the absolute injunction against hurting others to be an inadequate guide to resolving the actual dilemmas she faced. Her discovery of the disparity between intention and consequence and of the actual constraints of choice led her to realize that there is, in some situations, no way not to hurt. In confronting such dilemmas in both her personal and professional life, she does not abdicate responsibility for choice but rather claims the right to include herself among the people whom she considers it moral not to hurt. Her more inclusive morality now contains the injunction to be true to herself, leaving her with two principles of judgment whose integration she cannot yet clearly envision. What she does recognize is that both integrity and care must be included in a morality that can encompass the dilemmas of love and work that arise in adult life.

The move toward tolerance that accompanies the abandonment of absolutes is considered by William Perry (1968) to chart the course of intellectual and ethical development during the early adult years. Perry describes the changes in thinking that mark the transition from a belief that knowledge is absolute and answers clearly right or wrong to an understanding of the contextual relativity of both truth and choice. This transition and its impact on moral judgment can be discerned in the changes in moral understanding that occur in both men and women during the five years following college (Gilligan and Murphy, 1979; Murphy and Gilligan, 1980). Though both sexes move away from absolutes in this time, the absolutes themselves differ for each. In women's development, the absolute of care, defined initially as not hurting others, becomes complicated through a recognition of the need for personal integrity. This recognition gives rise to the claim for equality embodied in the concept of rights, which changes the understanding of relationships and transforms the definition of care. For men, the absolutes of truth and fairness, defined by the concepts of equality and reciprocity, are called into question by experiences that demonstrate the existence of differences between other and self. Then the awareness of multiple truths leads to a relativizing of equality in the direction of equity and gives rise to an ethic of generosity and care. For both sexes the existence of two contexts for moral decision makes judgment by definition contextually relative and leads to a new understanding of responsibility and choice.

The discovery of the reality of differences and thus of the contextual nature of morality and truth is described by Alex, a lawyer in the college student study, who began in law school "to realize that you really don't know everything" and "you don't ever know that there is any absolute. I don't think that you ever know that there is an absolute right. What you do know is you have to come down one way or the other. You have got to make a decision."

The awareness that he did not know everything arose more painfully in a relationship whose ending took him completely by surprise. In his belated discovery that the woman's experience had differed from his own, he realized how distant he had been in a relationship he considered close. Then the logical hierarchy of moral values, whose absolute truth he formerly proclaimed, came to seem a barrier to intimacy rather than a fortress of personal integrity. As his conception of morality began to change, his thinking focused on issues of relationship, and his concern with injustice was complicated by a new understanding of human attachment. Describing "the principle of attachment" that began to inform his way of look-

ing at moral problems, Alex sees the need for morality to extend
beyond considerations of fairness to concern with relationships:

> People have real emotional needs to be attached to something,
> and equality doesn't give you attachment. Equality fractures
> society and places on every person the burden of standing on
> his own two feet.

Although "equality is a crisp thing that you could hang onto," it
alone cannot adequately resolve the dilemmas of choice that arise
in life. Given his new awareness of responsibility and of the actual
consequences of choice, Alex says: "You don't want to look at just
equality. You want to look at how people are going to be able to
handle their lives." Recognizing the need for two contexts for judgment, he nevertheless finds that their integration "is hard to work
through," since sometimes "no matter which way you go, somebody
is going to be hurt and somebody is going to be hurt forever."
Then, he says, "you have reached the point where there is an irre-
solvable conflict," and choice becomes a matter of "choosing the
victim" rather than enacting the good. With the recognition of the
responsibility that such choices entail, his judgment becomes more
attuned to the psychological and social consequences of action, to
the reality of people's lives in an historical world.

Thus, starting from very different points, from the different
ideologies of justice and care, the men and women in the study
come, in the course of becoming adult, to a greater understanding
of both points of view and thus to a greater convergence in judgment. Recognizing the dual contexts of justice and care, they realize
that judgment depends on the way in which the problem is framed.

But in this light, the conception of development itself also depends on the context in which it is framed, and the vision of maturity can be seen to shift when adulthood is portrayed by women
rather than men. When women construct the adult domain, the
world of relationships emerges and becomes the focus of attention
and concern. McClelland (1975), noting this shift in women's fantasies of power, observes that "women are more concerned than men
with both sides of an interdependent relationship" and are "quicker
to recognize their own interdependence" pp. 85–86). This focus on
interdependence is manifest in fantasies that equate power with giving and care. McClelland reports that while men represent powerful
activity as assertion and aggression, women in contrast portray acts

of nurturance as acts of strength. Considering his research on power to deal "in particular with the characteristics of maturity," he suggests that mature women and men may relate to the world in a different style.

That women differ in their orientation to power is also the theme of Jean Baker Miller's analysis. Focusing on relationships of dominance and subordination, she finds women's situation in these relationships to provide "a crucial key to understanding the psychological order." This order arises from the relationships of difference, between man and woman and parent and child, that create "the milieu—the family—in which the human mind as we know it has been formed" (1976, p. 1). Because these relationships of difference contain, in most instances, a factor of inequality, they assume a moral dimension pertaining to the way in which power is used. On this basis, Miller distinguishes between relationships of temporary and permanent inequality, the former representing the context of human development, the latter, the condition of oppression. In relationships of temporary inequality, such as parent and child or teacher and student, power ideally is used to foster the development that removes the initial disparity. In relationships of permanent inequality, power cements dominance and subordination, and oppression is rationalized by theories that "explain" the need for its continuation.

Miller, focusing in this way on the dimension of inequality in human life, identifies the distinctive psychology of women as arising from the combination of their positions in relationships of temporary and permanent inequality. Dominant in temporary relationships of nurturance that dissolve with the dissolution of inequality, women are subservient in relationships of permanently unequal social status and power. In addition, though subordinate in social position to men, women are at the same time centrally entwined with them in the intimate and intense relationships of adult sexuality and family life. Thus women's psychology reflects both sides of relationships of interdependence and the range of moral possibilities to which such relationships give rise. Women, therefore, are ideally situated to observe the potential in human connection both for care and for oppression.

This distinct observational perspective informs the work of Carol Stack (1975) and Lillian Rubin (1976) who, entering worlds previously known through men's eyes, return to give a different report. In the urban black ghetto, where others have seen social disorder and family disarray, Stack finds networks of domestic exchange that describe the organization of the black family in poverty. Rubin, observing the families of the white working class, dispels the myth of "the affluent and happy worker" by charting the "worlds of pain" that it costs to raise a family in conditions of social and economic disadvantage. Both women describe an adulthood of relationships that sustain the family functions of protection and care, but also a social system of relationships that sustain economic dependence and social subordination. Thus they indicate how class, race, and ethnicity are used to justify and rationalize the continuing inequality of an economic system that benefits some at others' expense.

In their separate spheres of analysis, these women find order where others saw chaos—in the psychology of women, the urban black family, and the reproduction of social class. These discoveries required new modes of analysis and a more ethnographic approach in order to derive constructs that could give order and meaning to the adult life they saw. Until Stack redefined "family" as "the smallest organized, durable network of kin and non-kin who interact daily, providing the domestic needs of children and assuring their survival," she could not find "families" in the world of "The Flats." Only the "culturally specific definitions of certain concepts such as family, kin, parent, and friend that emerged during this study made much of the subsequent analysis possible ... An arbitrary imposition of widely accepted definitions of the family ... blocks the way to understanding how people in The Flats describe and order the world in which they live" (p. 31).

Similarly, Miller calls for "a new psychology of women" that recognizes the different starting point for women's development, the fact that "women stay with, build on, and develop in a context of attachment and affiliation with others," that "women's sense of self becomes very much organized around being able to make, and then to maintain, affiliations and relationships," and that "eventually, for many women, the threat of disruption of an affiliation is perceived not just as a loss of a relationship but as something closer to a total loss of self." Although this psychic structuring is by now familiar from descriptions of women's psychopathology, it has not been recognized that "this psychic starting point contains the possibilities for an entirely different (and more advanced) approach to living and functioning ... [in which] affiliation is valued as highly as, or more highly than, self-enhancement" (p. 83). Thus, Miller points to a psychology of adulthood which recognizes that development does not displace the value of ongoing attachment and the continuing importance of care in relationships.

The limitations of previous standards of measurement and the need for a more contextual mode of interpretation are evident as well in Rubin's approach. Rubin dispels the illusion that family life is everywhere the same or that subcultural differences can be assessed independently of the socioeconomic realities of class. Thus, working-class families "reproduce themselves not because they are somehow deficient or their culture aberrant, but because there are no alternatives for most of their children," despite "the mobility myth we cherish so dearly" (pp. 210–211). The temporary inequality of the working-class child thus turns into the permanent inequality of the working-class adult, caught in an ebb-tide of social mobility that erodes the quality of family life.

Like the stories that delineate women's fantasies of power, women's descriptions of adulthood convey a different sense of its social reality. In their portrayal of relationships, women replace the bias of men toward separation with a representation of the interdependence of self and other, both in love and in work. By changing the lens of developmental observation from individual achievement to relationships of care, women depict ongoing attachment as the path that leads to maturity. Thus the parameters of development shift toward marking the progress of affiliative relationship.

The implications of this shift are evident in considering the situation of women at mid-life. Given the tendency to chart the unfamiliar waters of adult development with the familiar markers of adolescent separation and growth, the middle years of women's lives readily appear as a time of return to the unfinished business of adolescence. This interpretation has been particularly compelling since life-cycle descriptions, derived primarily from studies of men, have generated a perspective from which women, insofar as they differ, appear deficient in their development. The deviance of female development has been especially marked in the adolescent years when girls appear to confuse identity with intimacy by defining themselves through relationships with others. The legacy left from this mode of identity definition is considered to be a self that is vulnerable to the issues of separation that arise at mid-life.

But this construction reveals the limitation in an account which measures women's development against a male standard and ignores the possibility of a different truth. In this light, the observation that women's embeddedness in lives of relationship, their orientation to interdependence, their subordination of achievement to care, and their conflicts over competitive success leave them personally at risk in mid-life seems more a commentary on the society than a problem in women's development.

The construction of mid-life in adolescent terms, as a similar crisis of identity and separation, ignores the reality of what has happened in the years between and tears up the history of love and of work. For generativity to begin at mid-life, as Vaillant's data on men suggest, seems from a woman's perspective too late for both sexes, given that the bearing and raising of children take place primarily in the preceeding years. Similarly, the image of women arriving at mid-life childlike and dependent on others is belied by the activity of their care in nurturing and sustaining family relationships. Thus the problem appears to be one of construction, an issue of judgment rather than truth.

In view of the evidence that women perceive and construe social reality differently from men and that these differences center around experiences of attachment and separation, life transitions that invariably engage these experiences can be expected to involve women in a distinctive way. And because women's sense of integrity appears to be entwined with an ethic of care, so that to see themselves as women is to see themselves in a relationship of connection, the major transitions in women's lives would seem to involve changes in the understanding and activities of care. Certainly the shift from childhood to adulthood witnesses a major redefinition of care. When the distinction between helping and pleasing frees the activity of taking care from the wish for approval by others, the ethic of responsibility can become a self-chosen anchor of personal integrity and strength.

In the same vein, however, the events of mid-life—the menopause and changes in family and work—can alter a woman's activities of care in ways that affect her sense of herself. If mid-life brings an end to relationships, to the sense of connection on which she relies, as well as to the activities of care through which she judges her worth, then the mourning that accompanies all life transitions can give way to the melancholia of self-deprecation and despair. The meaning of mid-life events for a woman thus reflects the interaction between the structures of her thought and the realities of her life.

When a distinction between neurotic and real conflict is made and the reluctance to choose is differentiated from the reality of having no choice, then it becomes possible to see more clearly how women's experience provides a key to understanding central truths of adult life. Rather than viewing her anatomy as destined to leave her with a scar of inferiority (Freud, 1931), one can see instead how it gives rise to experiences which illuminate a reality common to both of the sexes: the fact that in life you never see it all, that things unseen undergo change through time, that there is more than one path to gratification, and that the boundaries between self and other are less clear than they sometimes seem.

Thus women not only reach mid-life with a psychological history different from men's and face at that time a different social reality having different possibilities for love and for work, but they also make a different sense of experience, based on their knowledge of human relationships. Since the reality of connection is experienced by women as given rather than as freely contracted, they arrive at an understanding of life that reflects the limits of autonomy and control. As a result, women's development delineates the path not only to a less violent life but also to a maturity realized through interdependence and taking care.

In his studies of children's moral judgment, Piaget (1932/1965) describes a three-stage progression through which constraint turns into cooperation and cooperation into generosity. In doing so, he points out how long it takes before children in the same class at school, playing with each other every day, come to agree in their understanding of the rules of their games. This agreement, however, signals the completion of a major reorientation of action and thought through which the morality of constraint turns into the morality of cooperation. But he also notes how children's recognition of differences between others and themselves leads to a relativizing of equality in the direction of equity, signifying a fusion of justice and love.

There seems at present to be only partial agreement between men and women about the adulthood they commonly share. In the absence of mutual understanding, relationships between the sexes continue in varying degrees of constraint, manifesting the "paradox of egocentrism" which Piaget describes, a mystical respect for rules combined with everyone playing more or less as he pleases and paying no attention to his neighbor (p. 61). For a life-cycle understanding to address the development in adulthood of relationships characterized by cooperation, generosity, and care, that understanding must include the lives of women as well as of men.

Among the most pressing items on the agenda for research on adult development is the need to delineate *in women's own terms* the experience of their adult life. My own work in that direction indicates that the inclusion of women's experience brings to developmental understanding a new perspective on relationships that changes the basic constructs of interpretation. The concept of identity expands to include the experience of interconnection. The moral domain is similarly enlarged by the inclusion of responsibility and care in relationships. And the underlying epistemology correspondingly shifts from the Greek ideal of knowledge as a correspondence between mind and form to the Biblical conception of knowing as a process of human relationship.

Given the evidence of different perspectives in the representation of adulthood by women and men, there is a need for research that elucidates the effects of these differences in marriage, family, and work relationships. My research suggests that men and women may speak different languages that they assume are the same, using similar words to encode disparate experiences of self and social relationships. Because these languages share an overlapping moral vocabulary, they contain a propensity for systematic mistranslation, creating misunderstandings which impede communication and limit the potential for cooperation and care in relationships. At the same time, however, these languages articulate with one another in critical ways. Just as the language of responsibilities provides a weblike imagery of relationships to replace a hierarchical ordering that dissolves with the coming of equality, so the language of rights underlines the importance of including in the network of care not only the other but also the self.

As we have listened for centuries to the voices of men and the theories of development that their experience informs, so we have come more recently to notice not only the silence of women but the difficulty in hearing what they say when they speak. Yet in the different voice of women lies the truth of an ethic of care, the tie between relationship and responsibility, and the origins of aggression in the failure of connection. The failure to see the different reality of women's lives and to hear the differences in their voices stems in part from the assumption that there is a single mode of social experience and interpretation. By positing instead two different modes, we arrive at a more complex rendition of human experience which sees the truth of separation and attachment in the lives of women and men and recognizes how these truths are carried by different modes of language and thought.

To understand how the tension between responsibilities and rights sustains the dialectic of human development is to see the integrity of two disparate modes of experience that are in the end connected. While an ethic of justice proceeds from the premise of equality—that everyone should be treated the same—an ethic of care rests on the premise of nonviolence—that no one should be hurt. In the representation of maturity, both perspectives converge in the realization that just as inequality adversely affects both parties in an unequal relationship, so too violence is destructive for everyone involved. This dialogue between fairness and care not only provides a better understanding of relations between the sexes but also gives rise to a more comprehensive portrayal of adult work and family relationships.

As Freud and Piaget call our attention to the differences in children's feelings and thought, enabling us to respond to children with greater care and respect, so a recognition of the differences in women's experience and understanding expands our vision of maturity and points to the contextual nature of developmental truths. Through this expansion in perspective, we can begin to envision how a marriage between adult development as it is currently portrayed and women's development as it begins to be seen could lead to a changed understanding of human development and a more generative view of human life.

References
Index

References

Belenky, Mary F. "Conflict and Development: A Longitudinal Study of the Impact of Abortion Decisions on Moral Judgments of Adolescent and Adult Women." PhD. Diss., Harvard University, 1978.

Bergling, Kurt. *Moral Development: The Validity of Kohlberg's Theory.* Stockholm Studies in Educational Psychology 23. Stockholm, Sweden· Almqvist and Wiksell International, 1981.

Bergman, Ingmar. *Wild Strawberries* (1957). In *Four Screen Plays of Ingmar Bergman,* trans. Lars Malmstrom and David Kushner. New York: Simon and Schuster, 1960.

Bettelheim, Bruno. "The Problem of Generations." In E. Erikson, ed., *The Challenge of Youth.* New York: Doubleday, 1965.

———. *The Uses of Enchantment.* New York: Alfred A. Knopf, 1976.

Blos, Peter. "The Second Individuation Process of Adolescence." In A. Freud, ed., *The Psychoanalytic Study of the Child,* vol. 22. New York: International Universities Press, 1967.

Broverman, I., Vogel, S., Broverman, D., Clarkson, F., and Rosenkrantz, P. "Sex-role Stereotypes: A Current Appraisal." *Journal of Social Issues* 28 (1972): 59–78.

Chekhov, Anton. *The Cherry Orchard* (1904). In *Best Plays by Chekhov,* trans. Stark Young. New York: The Modern Library, 1956.

Chodorow, Nancy. "Family Structure and Feminine Personality." In M. Z. Rosaldo and L. Lamphere, eds., *Woman, Culture and Society.* Stanford: Stanford University Press, 1974.

———. *The Reproduction of Mothering.* Berkeley: University of California Press, 1978.

Coles, Robert. *Children of Crisis.* Boston: Little, Brown, 1964.

Didion, Joan. "The Women's Movement." *New York Times Book Review,* July 30, 1972, pp. 1–2, 14.

Douvan, Elizabeth, and Adelson, Joseph. *The Adolescent Experience.* New York· John Wiley and Sons, 1966

Drabble, Margaret. *The Waterfall*. Hammondsworth, Eng.: Penguin Books, 1969.

Edwards, Carolyn P. "Societal Complexity and Moral Development: A Kenyan Study." *Ethos* 3 (1975): 505–527.

Eliot, George. *The Mill on the Floss* (1860). New York: New American Library, 1965.

Erikson, Erik H. *Childhood and Society*. New York: W. W. Norton, 1950.

———. *Young Man Luther*. New York: W. W. Norton, 1958.

———. *Insight and Responsibility*. New York: W. W. Norton, 1964.

———. *Identity: Youth and Crisis*. New York: W. W. Norton, 1968.

———. *Gandhi's Truth*. New York: W. W. Norton, 1969.

———. "Reflections on Dr. Borg's Life Cycle." *Daedalus 105* (1976): 1–29. (Also in Erikson, ed., *Adulthood*. New York: W. W. Norton, 1978.)

Freud, Sigmund. *The Standard Edition of the Complete Psychological Works of Sigmund Freud*, trans. and ed. James Strachey. London: The Hogarth Press 1961.

———. *Three Essays on the Theory of Sexuality* (1905). Vol. VII.

———. "Civilized Sexual Morality and Modern Nervous Illness" (1908). Vol. IX.

———. "On Narcissism: An Introduction" (1914). Vol. XIV.

———. "Some Psychical Consequences of the Anatomical Distinction Between the Sexes" (1925). Vol. XIX.

———. *The Question of Lay Analysis* (1926). Vol. XX.

———. *Civilization and Its Discontents* (1930/1929). Vol. XXI.

———. "Female Sexuality" (1931). Vol. XXI.

———. *New Introductory Lectures on Psycho-analysis. (1933/1932)*. Vol. XXII.

Gilligan, Carol, "Moral Development in the College Years." In A. Chickering, ed., *The Modern American College*. San Francisco: Jossey-Bass, 1981.

Gilligan, Carol, and Belenky, Mary F. "A Naturalistic Study of Abortion Decisions." In R. Selman and R. Yando, eds., *Clinical-Developmental Psychology*. New Directions for Child Development, no. 7. San Francisco: Jossey-Bass, 1980.

Gilligan, Carol, and Murphy, John Michael. "Development from Adolescence to Adulthood: The Philosopher and the 'Dilemma of the Fact.' " In D. Kuhn, ed., *Intellectual Development Beyond Childhood*. New Directions for Child Development, no. 5. San Francisco: Jossey-Bass, 1979.

Haan, Norma. "Hypothetical and Actual Moral Reasoning in a Situation of Civil Disobedience." *Journal of Personality and Social Psychology* 32 (1975): 255–270.

Holstein, Constance. "Development of Moral Judgment: A Longitudinal Study of Males and Females." *Child Development* 47 (1976): 51–61.

Horner, Matina S. "Sex Differences in Achievement Motivation and Performance in Competitive and Noncompetitive Situations." Ph.D. Diss., University of Michigan, 1968. University Microfilms #6912135.

———. "Toward an Understanding of Achievement-related Conflicts in Women." *Journal of Social Issues* 28 (1972): 157–175.

Ibsen, Henrik. *A Doll's House* (1879). In *Ibsen Plays*, trans. Peter Watts. Hammondsworth, Eng.: Penguin Books, 1965.

Joyce, James. *A Portrait of the Artist as a Young Man* (1916). New York: The Viking Press, 1956.

Kingston, Maxine Hong. *The Woman Warrior*. New York: Alfred A. Knopf, 1977.

Kohlberg, Lawrence. "The Development of Modes of Thinking and Choices in Years 10 to 16." Ph.D. Diss., University of Chicago, 1958.

———. "Stage and Sequence: The Cognitive-Development Approach to Socialization." In D. A. Goslin, ed., *Handbook of Socialization Theory and Research*. Chicago: Rand McNally, 1969.

———. "Continuities and Discontinuities in Childhood and Adult Moral Development Revisited." In *Collected Papers on Moral Development and Moral Education*. Moral Education Research Foundation, Harvard University, 1973.

———. "Moral Stages and Moralization: The Cognitive-Developmental Approach." In T. Lickona, ed., *Moral Development and Behavior: Theory, Research and Social Issues*. New York: Holt, Rinehart and Winston, 1976.

———. *The Philosophy of Moral Development*. San Francisco: Harper and Row, 1981.

Kohlberg, L., and Gilligan, C. "The Adolescent as a Philosopher: The Discovery of the Self in a Post-conventional World." *Daedalus* 100 (1971): 1051–1086.

Kohlberg, L., and Kramer, R. "Continuities and Discontinuities in Child and Adult Moral Development." *Human Development* 12 (1969): 93–120.

Langdale, Sharry, and Gilligan, Carol. Interim Report to the National Institute of Education. 1980.

Lever, Janet. "Sex Differences in the Games Children Play." *Social Problems* 23 (1976): 478–487.

———. "Sex Differences in the Complexity of Children's Play and Games." *American Sociological Review* 43 (1978): 471–483.

Levinson, Daniel J. *The Seasons of a Man's Life*. New York: Alfred A. Knopf, 1978

Loevinger, Jane, and Wessler, Ruth. *Measuring Ego Development*. San Francisco: Jossey-Bass, 1970.

Lyons, Nona. "Seeing the Consequences: The Dialectic of Choice and Reflectivity in Human Development." Qualifying Paper, Graduate School of Education, Harvard University, 1980.

Maccoby, Eleanor, and Jacklin, Carol. *The Psychology of Sex Differences*. Stanford: Stanford University Press, 1974.

May, Robert. *Sex and Fantasy*. New York: W. W. Norton, 1980.

McCarthy, Mary. *Memories of a Catholic Girlhood*. New York: Harcourt Brace Jovanovich, 1946.

McClelland, David C. *Power: The Inner Experience*. New York: Irvington, 1975.

McClelland, D. C., Atkinson, J. W., Clark, R. A., and Lowell, E. L. *The Achievement Motive*. New York: Irvington, 1953.

Mead, George Herbert. *Mind, Self, and Society*. Chicago: Univeristy of Chicago Press, 1934.

Miller, Jean Baker. *Toward a New Psychology of Women*. Boston: Beacon Press, 1976.

Murphy, J. M., and Gilligan, C. "Moral Development in Late Adolescence and Adulthood: A Critique and Reconstruction of Kohlberg's Theory." *Human Development* 23 (1980): 77–104.

Perry, William. *Forms of Intellectual and Ethical Development in the College Years.* New York: Holt, Rinehart and Winston, 1968.

Piaget, Jean. *The Moral Judgment of the Child* (1932). New York: The Free Press, 1965.

———. *Six Psychological Studies.* New York: Viking Books, 1968.

———. *Structuralism.* New York: Basic Books, 1970.

Pollak, Susan, and Gilligan, Carol. "Images of Violence in Thematic Apperception Test Stories." *Journal of Personality and Social Psychology* 42, no. 1 (1982): 159–167.

Rubin, Lillian. *Worlds of Pain.* New York: Basic Books, 1976.

Sassen, Georgia. "Success Anxiety in Women: A Constructivist Interpretation of Its Sources and Its Significance." *Harvard Educational Review* 50 (1980): 13–25.

Schneir, Miriam, ed., *Feminism: The Essential Historical Writings.* New York: Vintage Books, 1972.

Simpson, Elizabeth L. "Moral Development Research: A Case Study of Scientific Cultural Bias." *Human Development* 17 (1974): 81–106.

Stack, Carol B. *All Our Kin.* New York: Harper and Row, 1974.

Stoller, Robert, J. "A Contribution to the Study of Gender Identity." *International Journal of Psycho-Analysis* 45 (1964): 220–226.

Strunk, William Jr., and White, E. B. *The Elements of Style* (1918). New York: Macmillan, 1958.

Terman, L., and Tyler, L. "Psychological Sex Differences." In L. Carmichael, ed., *Manual of Child Psychology.* 2nd ed. New York: John Wiley and Sons, 1954.

Tolstoy, Sophie A. *The Diary of Tolstoy's Wife, 1860–1891,* trans. Alexander Werth, London: Victor Gollancz, 1928. (Also in M. J. Moffat and C. Painter, eds., *Revelations.* New York: Vintage Books, 1975.)

Vaillant, George E. *Adaptation to Life.* Boston: Little, Brown, 1977.

Whiting, Beatrice, and Pope, Carolyn. "A Cross-cultural Analysis of Sex Difference in the Behavior of Children Age Three to Eleven." *Journal of Social Psychology* 91 (1973): 171–188.

Woolf, Virginia. *A Room of One's Own.* New York: Harcourt, Brace and World, 1929.

Index
of
Study
Participants

General
Index